Twayne's United States Authors Series

Sylvia E. Bowman, *Editor*

INDIANA UNIVERSITY

Seba Smith

TUSAS 283

Ambrotype of Seba Smith

SEBA SMITH

By MILTON and PATRICIA RICKELS
University of Southwestern Louisiana

TWAYNE PUBLISHERS

A DIVISION OF G. K. HALL & CO., BOSTON

Library of Congress Cataloging in Publication Data

Rickels, Milton.
  Seba Smith.

  (Twayne's United States authors series; TUSAS 283)
  Bibliography: p. 161-64.
  Includes index.
  1.   Smith, Seba, 1792-1868—Criticism and interpre-
tation.   I.   Rickels, Patricia, 1927-   joint author.
PS2877.R5   818'.3'07   77-4830
ISBN 0-8057-7185-0

PS
2877
R5

***

"In a nascent culture such as ours, peaks of achievement have occurred and must have their place, but if our concern is with the whole dimensional pattern minor figures may also become symbols of a dominant creative effort."

— Constance Rourke,
The Roots of American Culture

Contents

About the Authors

Patricia and Milton Rickels are Professors of English at the University of Southwestern Louisiana. She earned the B. A. degree from the University of Washington, Seattle; he, from California State University, Fresno. Both hold the Ph. D. from the Louisiana State University. They teach courses in American Literature, American folklore, and American humor. Both past presidents of the Louisiana Folklore Society, they serve as co-editors of the *Louisiana Folklore Miscellany.*

Patricia Rickels's publications include a series of articles in the *Louisiana Folklore Miscellany,* a chapter, "Memories of Lead Belly," in J. Mason Brewer's *American Negro Folklore* (1968), and the essay "The Folklore of Acadiana" in Steven Del Sesto and Jon L. Gibson's *The Culture of Acadiana* (1975). She and her husband co-authored the monograph *Richard Wright* (1970).

Milton Rickels has published *Thomas Bangs Thorpe: Humorist of the Old Southwest* (1962), *George Washington Harris,* (TUSAS 91, 1965), and essays and reviews in *American Literature, Criticism, The Southern Review, The Lovingood Papers* and elsewhere.

Preface

Modern readers can hardly recapture the excitement of Seba Smith's contemporaries over his Downing letters. Newspaper publication assured that each letter would be separately received, that there would be time for it to be savored, mulled over, probably read aloud. Topical allusions and timely jokes could be recognized and explained by the informed. Readers got acquainted with Jack Downing a little at a time, as we do with real persons. The taste for his down east company grew strong among Americans who were still wondering exactly how they were different from Englishmen and where they were going as a nation. We imagine people waiting eagerly for Jack's next letter to see how he would respond to the events of the day. Quite likely, many who in 1833 bought *The Life and Writings of Major Jack Downing* and later *My Thirty Years Out of the Senate* did so to enjoy again their first delight in the letters.

Today's reader encountering a volume of the Downing letters is faced with a far different experience: here is writing from long ago, from the early days of the Republic. Letter follows letter in close-packed print that is without quotation marks and almost without paragraphing. There are allusions and suspected allusions to people and events long forgotten. Changing literary fashions and tastes make the letters seem slow moving, ponderous, murky. The present study endeavors, however, to help later readers understand and experience some of the original impact of these mock-rustic letters by explaining their historical and political context, by analyzing selected letters, and by stopping to examine and appreciate the details of style and meaning which contribute to the artistic whole.

Our organization is chronological: a first chapter summarizes those portions of Smith's early life and education significant in explaining his career as a writer—his deep roots in the folk culture and his devotion to higher education and literary culture. The following three chapters assess the colloquial style and detail the creation of Jack Downing's character as Smith developed it in the series of mock letters that he composed for his newspaper from early 1830 into 1833. Elements of pastoral innocence and beauty, of ignorance and foolishness, of aggressiveness and corrupting ambition in Jack's character are examined for their social and political significance to Seba Smith and to his readers.

Smith used Jack as a persona to comment about the consequences for American culture of the movement to mass democracy that Andrew Jackson's leadership encouraged. As Seba struggled to express his mistrust of the Jacksonian revolution, he turned increasingly to the themes and techniques of folk humor. The values and the esthetics of this ancient comic tradition provided Smith the perspective of a second culture, enabling him to evaluate the official culture to which he himself self-consciously belonged and which he consciously supported. Chapter 4 examines Smith's burlesques of several historical Jacksonian events to show how Smith's complex perspective endows them with a rich human fullness.

Chapter 5 examines the problems Smith faced in turning his letters into a book. To provide a basic structure, he created a burlesque campaign biography. Thus, his introductory essay, "My Life," is discussed at this point because it was written after he had experimented with his character for over two years. Consequently, as an artistic creation, this essay represents a late, shaping definition of his fictional character. Coming first in Smith's book, then, the mock biography operates esthetically to present the richness of Jack's folk culture, his marvelous vitality, and at the same time his comic incapacity in politics or anywhere outside his little community.

The following three chapters—6, 7, and 8—cover Smith's early New York years as an editor and as a nationally popular author. In *John Smith's Letters with "Picters" to Match*, Seba continues his examination of the folk culture and also reveals his private embarrassments over his commonplace last name. Chapter 7 analyzes the intentions, the sources, and the badly flawed poetics, so mercilessly ridiculed by Edgar Allan Poe, of *Powhatan*, Smith's most self-consciously ambitious creative effort. Here, too, his uninformed excursion into higher mathematics is outlined. Finally, Smith's magazine verse is analyzed for its quality and for clues to its immense popularity.

Chapter 9 argues that Smith's volume of New England tales, *'Way Down East* (1854), is, next to the Downing letters, his most creative achievement. The tales are grouped and examined for their esthetic qualities and for their historical and folkloric content. Although often structurally flawed, the stories present a significant

Preface

achievement. The informing idea is that the New England rustic life of the not too distant past was a Golden Age of vital people, fruitful work, and joyful play. The Yankee characters are not the grim, close, stereotyped figures of popular literature; they are varied types who are frequently generous, unselfish, and richly affectionate. Again, as in the Downing letters, Smith contributes to one of the grand themes of American literature—the innocence and beauty of New World man.

Chapter 10 examines Smith's final use of the Jack Downing figure to satirize American domestic politics and foreign policy for the Washington *National Intelligencer*. The final chapter assesses Smith's place in our national literature and concludes that his major contribution was in laying the groundwork for a genuinely vernacular perspective and colloquial style.

MILTON AND PATRICIA RICKELS

University of Southwestern Louisiana
Lafayette, Louisiana

Acknowledgments

It is a pleasure to thank the many people who have helped us with this book. More librarians than we can list have assisted us in finding materials in their collections, arranged for the photocopying of rare items, and given permission for us to quote from documents in their archives. Special thanks go to Miss Anne Freudenberg, Curator of Manuscripts, Mr. Eaves, and Miss Carver at the Alderman Library, University of Virginia, for help with boxes of manuscripts. At the Maine Historical Society Library in Portland, Miss Elizabeth Ring went through stacks of material for us, and Mr. Earle Shettleworth located an ambrotype of Seba Smith and arranged for its reproduction. Mr. Robert W. Hill, Keeper of Manuscripts at the New York Public Library, located material and granted us a variety of courtesies.

Miss Carolyn Jakeman of the Houghton Library at Harvard found documents relating Elizabeth Oakes Smith to other literary figures of her time. Mr. Robert L. Volz, Special Collections, Bowdoin College Library, located a valuable manuscript autobiography of Seba Smith and arranged to lend us two rare books. Mrs. Davis of Haverford College checked their Charles Roberts Autograph Collection for us; and archivists at Yale, the University of Pennsylvania, and the University of North Carolina libraries helped us examine their collections. Mr. Kenin of the Pennsylvania Historical Society found useful material among their Griswold papers.

Various persons have shared their special expertise. M. Daniel Royot of the Institut d'Anglais, Université de Clermont-Ferrand, gave us a copy of his unpublished checklist of Smith's publications in Portland, Maine, newspapers from 1813 to 1836—the fruits of painstaking research. Dean David Tatham of Syracuse University sent us information about Smith's first illustrator, David Claypoole Johnston, and explained certain matters of technique in nineteenth-century American graphic art. Professor Cameron Nickels of Madison College shared items of information and discussed points of interpretation with us. Our colleagues Professors Duane Blumberg and James H. Dorman evaluated Smith's contribution to geometry for us and told us what books to read about Jacksonian

Acknowledgements

America. The Honorable Edgar G. Mouton of the Louisiana Senate commented on legislative burlesques and mock proceedings as he knew them. Mrs. Joy Oaksmith Barnacastle, a great-granddaughter of Seba Smith, sent us copies of items and details of family history. For permission to quote from letters and manuscripts, our thanks go to Mr. Edmund Berkeley, Jr., Curator of Manuscripts, Alderman Library of the University of Virginia, for materials from the Elizabeth Oakes Smith Collection; to Mr. Richard Harwell, Librarian, for Bowdoin College materials; and to Ms. Faye Simkin, Executive Officer, for permission to quote from the Seba Smith Miscellaneous Papers, Manuscripts and Archives Division, The New York Public Library, Astor, Lenox, and Tilden Foundations.

For permissions to quote copyrighted work, we thank Harcourt, Brace, Jovanovich for passages from Constance Rourke's *The Roots of American Culture;* and Random House, Inc., Alfred A. Knopf, Inc., for passages from H. L. Mencken's *The American Language, Supplement One,* and from Alexis de Tocqueville's *Democracy in America,* translated by Henry Reeve, revised by Francis Bowen, and edited by Phillips Bradley.

All scholars owe gratitude to members of the American Association of University Presses for encouraging authors to quote from their publications, within the doctrine of fair use, without prior permission. From this group we thank the Massachusetts Institute of Technology Press for passages from Mikhail Bakhtin's *Rabelais and His World,* translated by Helene Iswolsky; the Louisiana State University Press for a quotation from Lewis P. Simpson's *The Man of Letters in New England and the South;* the Oxford University Press for passages from Leo Marx's *The Machine in the Garden,* John William Ward's *Andrew Jackson: Symbol for an Age,* and Daniel Hoffman's *Form and Fable in American Fiction;* and the Princeton University Press for material from Miguel de Unamuno's *The Life of Don Quixote and Sancho,* translated by Anthony Kerrigan.

We are grateful for the support of Dean Mary E. Dichmann and to the University of Southwestern Louisiana for granting us both sabbatical leave to do research in Maine and at various libraries in the summer of 1965.

To Dr. Sylvia E. Bowman we wish to express our thanks for inviting us to undertake this study and for being generous in granting us extensions of time to complete it.

All subsequent students of Seba Smith will be indebted, as we are, to Miss Mary Alice Wyman's *Two American Pioneers*, which has been our constant guide in research. She has so well performed the basic and difficult critical task of separating the genuine from the spurious Downing letters that we have merely alluded to her results. The interested student is referred to her Chapter IV.

Chronology

1792   Seba Smith born September 14, in Buckfield, Maine.

1797   Family moves to Turner, Maine, which later became the model for Smith's fictional Downingville.

1799   Family moves to Bridgton, Maine; Seba picks up a little schooling and works at odd jobs.

1810   Begins teaching in district schools while attending part-time North Bridgton Academy

1815   Enters Bowdoin College as a sophomore.

1818   Graduates at the head of his class. Moves to Portland where he teaches for a year and publishes several poems.

1819   Travels to South Carolina and then across the Atlantic to Liverpool. Upon his return to Portland, becomes assistant editor of the *Eastern Argus*, a position he holds for several years.

1823   Marries seventeen-year-old Elizabeth Oakes Prince.

1829   Starts a weekly paper, the *Family Reader,* and the *Portland Courier,* the first daily paper north and east of Boston.

1830   Publishes on January 18, in the *Portland Courier,* the first of a series of rustic letters purporting to be the compositions of Jack Downing, of Downingville, a down East youth. During the year publishes a doggerel poem on the life and death of the folk hero Sam Patch.

1833   Imitations of the Downing letters begin to appear. In October, Charles Augustus Davis, the most successful imitator, asserts his authorship of all the letters. In November, Smith's book *The Life and Writings of Major Jack Downing* is published in Boston.

1834   Second edition of *The Life and Writings of Major Jack Downing.* On July 4 Smith begins publication, under the name Jack Downing, of the weekly *Downing Gazette,* devoted to political matters.

1836   Jack's death and funeral are reported in the *Downing Gazette* on March 22.

1837   Through unsuccessful speculation in wilderness land, Smith loses his interest in the *Portland Courier*.

1839   Writes for the New York *Mirror* a series of comic letters which are published in book form in May as *John Smith's Letters with "Picters" to Match*. Settles in New York City, where Seba and Elizabeth both find a market for their writing in the popular magazines and giftbooks and become minor members of the literati.

1840   A letter in the *New World* announces the resurrection and marriage of Major Downing.

1841   *Powhatan; A Metrical Romance* published.

1842   *The Sinless Child*, a long poem by Mrs. Smith, achieves great success. She begins signing herself Elizabeth Oaksmith or Oakes Smith.

1843-   Smith edits *Rover*, for which he writes occasional Major
1845   Downing letters, and, on December 28, 1843, "A Corpse Going to a Ball," which is to pass into the oral tradition as the ballad, "Fair Charlotte." Also edits the *New York Citizen and American Republican*.

1845   *May-Day in New-York* published in Philadelphia. Smith edits the giftbook *Dewdrops of the Nineteenth Century*.

1846   Publishes six articles on "The Religion and Superstitions of the North American Indians" in *The Literary Emporium*.

1846-   Last series of Smith's Downing letters appears in the
1856   Washington, D.C., *National Intelligencer*.

1850   Smith publishes what he considers his most significant work, *New Elements of Geometry*.

1851   Elizabeth begins a career as public lecturer and becomes the family's chief financial support.

1853   Smith begins publication of a comic paper, *Budget*.

1854   His collected stories are published as *'Way Down East; or, Portraitures of Yankee Life*.

1854-   Edits the *United States Magazine* and *United States Jour-*
1859   *nal*, furnishing material for both publications.

1857   Takes over *Emerson's United States Magazine and Putnam's Monthly*. A financial failure, the magazine stops publication after one year.

1859   *My Thirty Years Out of the Senate* by Major Jack Downing reprints what Smith considers the best of the Downing letters. Edits the short-lived magazine *The Great Republic*.

1860	Moves to Patchogue, Long Island. Growing deafness causes Smith to live in retirement.
1862	Last series of spurious Downing letters begins in the New York *Weekly Caucasian*. Collected in 1864 as *Letters of Major Jack Downing of the Downingville Militia*, they are personal and vulgar satires about Abraham Lincoln.
1867	Smith becomes seriously ill, partially paralyzed.
1868	On July 28 dies and is buried in Patchogue, New York.
1893	After twenty-five years of widowhood spent in writing and lecturing, Elizabeth dies in North Carolina.
1927	Mary Alice Wyman publishes *Two American Pioneers: Seba Smith and Elizabeth Oakes Smith*.

CHAPTER 1

A Down East Life

SEBA Smith is known to students of American literature and history as the creator of Jack Downing, the Yankee character who became a household word as the personification of the rising common man in the age of Jacksonian Democracy and who provided a model for the symbolic figure of Uncle Sam. Smith's origins were as archetypically American as Jack's. Born in a log cabin on the frontier, he grew up poor in a country village and became a self-made man of the sort America has prided itself upon producing.

As far back as family records went, Smith's ancestors had been Massachusetts people. In 1780 his grandfather and father moved "down east" to the township of Turner, Province of Maine. Seba Smith's father (also Seba), soon after his marriage to Apphia Stevens, moved even farther back into the wilderness, helping to establish the frontier settlement of Buckfield, Oxford County, by building a log cabin there. In this house their son Seba was born on September 14, 1792.[1]

I Yankee Boyhood

When the boy Seba was about six, his family moved back to Turner, the village which was to become the model for Smith's fictional Downingville,[2] and four or five years later to Bridgton in Cumberland County, some forty miles north of Portland. Bridgton provided some of the advantages of civilization: "the commonest of common schools and the scantiest and crudest school books of that day," a grocery store, a brickyard, and a small cast-iron foundry—in all of which Seba found part-time work during his boyhood. In spite of limited opportunities, he managed to scrape together enough learning so that he was considered qualified by the age of eighteen to teach in the district schools of Bridgton and neighboring towns.[3]

Already Smith was beginning to exhibit a hunger for education which sharply differentiates him from Jack Downing whose ambitions were for adventure and success rather than for intellectual enlightment. Seba eagerly welcomed the opening of Bridgton Academy, a good preparatory school, where he managed to obtain part-time instruction over a period of two years under the direction of Professor Bezaleel Cushman, who inspired in him the desire for a college education. Smith's family could never have afforded to send him to college; but in 1815, through the financial assistance of "a generous and philanthropic gentleman of Portland," he entered Bowdoin, as a twenty-three-year-old sophomore.[4]

II Education at Bowdoin

Situated in Brunswick, Maine, on a beautiful site near the falls of the Androscoggin, Bowdoin College had been open for just thirteen years but already had a reputation for high scholastic standards and was a matter for great pride in the state. Henry Wadsworth Longfellow's father, for instance, himself a Harvard graduate, sent both his sons there in 1822;[5] and Nathaniel Hawthorne was a member of the same class. Assessing the tone of Bowdoin for its influence on Hawthorne's development, Henry James says:

This institution was in the year 1821 . . . a highly honorable, but not a very elaborately organized, nor a particularly impressive seat of learning. . . . It was a homely, simple, frugal "country college," of the old-fashioned American stamp; exerting within its limits a civilizing influence, working, amid the forests and the lakes, the log-houses and clearings, toward the amenities and humanities and other collegiate graces, and offering a very sufficient education to the future lawyers, merchants, clergymen, politicians, and editors, of the very active and knowledge-loving community that supported it. It did more than this—it numbered poets and statesmen among its undergraduates.[6]

In a letter to classmate Horatio Bridge that was printed as the dedication of *The Snow-Image*, Hawthorne recalled that the amusements of the Bowdoin students had been "gathering blueberries in study-hours under those tall academic pines; or watching the great logs as they tumbled along the current of the Androscoggin; or shooting pigeons and gray squirrels in the woods; or bat-fowling in the summer twilight or catching trout. . . ." James comments that this is "a very pretty picture, but it is a picture of happy urchins at school, not of undergraduates." Clearly Bowdoin was a place where a young man could obtain education

without sophistication. It was, in James' words, "indeed thousands
of miles away from Oxford and Cambridge."[7]

Smith, who lived very frugally at college, prepared his own meals
to save money and returned to teaching during every vacation;[8] but
he did well in his studies and found time to take part in campus activities. Of the nineteen students in his class, most eventually entered the professions, four to become trustees or overseers of the
college; eleven earned masters' degrees and two doctors' degrees.
Smith was one of six members of the class elected to Phi Beta Kappa.[9] Like Longfellow, he was a member of Peucinian, Bowdoin's
first and most scholarly literary society, which had its own large and
well-selected library and which held regular meetings for the discussion of topics such as "whether the fear of shame or the love of
honor be the greater inducement to virtue." The members were
required to write and deliver various kinds of papers at meetings.[10]
Smith doubtless profited from this practice in writing and speaking
as well as from the privileges of the society's browsing room in
which current issues of good American and British periodicals were
available.[11] During his last term in college, his health was very poor;
he was unable to pursue all the regular studies with his class; nevertheless, he graduated with distinction and was invited to deliver a
valedictory oration at the commencement on September 8, 1818.[12]

III   *The Search for a Vocation*

After graduation Smith obtained a teaching position in a private
school in Portland and began to write poetry, some of which was
published in the local *Eastern Argus*. Because his health continued
to be poor, he decided at the completion of his first year of work to
take a long vacation trip to restore his strength. Taking his time and
walking at least part of the way, he traveled through the Atlantic
states as far as Charleston, South Carolina; he then booked passage
on a freighter for Liverpool. This period of leisure gave him time to
think about his future. Teaching did not seem his true vocation, and
he was encouraged by the popularity of some of his poetry, particularly a sentimental piece entitled "The Mother Perishing in a
Snowstorm," to believe he might find a career as a writer—possibly
as a member of the *Eastern Argus* staff. Fate took a hand in his affairs at this point, for when his ship docked in America, the first
news he heard was of the sudden death of the owner of the *Argus*
and the resulting confusion in the paper's affairs. Smith went at

once to the *Argus* office and secured the post of assistant editor. During the first year, he purchased a half-interest in the paper, and he continued as editor for four years.[13]

IV *Marriage*

Established now as a journalist, Smith could think about becoming a family man. On March 6, 1823, at the age of thirty-one, he married a beautiful, bright, ambitious, and strong-minded seventeen-year-old native of Cumberland, Maine—Miss Elizabeth Oakes Prince. An early exponent of women's liberation, Elizabeth had determined never to marry but to devote her life to teaching and study. She married in deference to the wishes of her mother who believed matrimony was the only proper career for a woman.[14] The Smiths' marriage, which lasted until Seba's death forty-four years later, was marked by rather unusual circumstances for the mid-nineteenth century.

In some ways Elizabeth seems to have been a model Victorian wife. She bore six sons, reared four to adulthood, and managed a household under often very trying circumstances. She cooperated with her husband in a number of literary ventures. Indeed, it required their combined efforts to support the family, as Smith indicated in a letter to Rufus W. Griswold in 1842. A pen, he said, was not a crutch but merely a staff; nevertheless, "since Mrs. Smith and myself have each a staff, if we walk together I hope we may be able to keep from falling."[15] Letters exchanged by Elizabeth and Seba over the years demonstrate a strong and enduring bond of affection. For example, a letter he sent to her in 1833 when he was in Boston, reading proof for his first book begins: "My dear companion, through the world's wide wilderness, I take my pen, having passed another day without seeing or speaking to you, upon whom I have looked and with whom I have conversed every day for ten years."[16] Their letters generally indicate real pleasure in each others' love and presence.

But there were unconventional aspects of the marriage and persistent rumors that the Smiths did not get along.[17] Elizabeth maintained a separate career as a writer, lecturer, and public personage who boldly espoused the controversial cause of women's rights. A handsome woman, she was as vivacious as Seba was retiring; and Poe, Griswold, Emerson, Longfellow—in fact most men—found her charming. She knew and corresponded with many of the prominent people of the era, not hesitating to address herself to governors and presidents. She traveled widely on speaking tours, left Seba at home to mind the children, and caused him on one occasion to write her a rather pathetic plea to send a little money for household expenses.[18]

Altogether, in her own time, Elizabeth eclipsed her husband in reputation, though none of her work is well-known today. Perhaps most interesting of all, she began after some years of marriage to use the name Oaksmith (a telescoping of her middle name Oakes with Smith) in her personal life and as a *nom de plume*. Eventually she had all the children's names legally changed to Oaksmith, and this rejection of his name was undoubtedly wounding to Smith. When he recounts this episode of the family history in his autobiography manuscript, his tone is matter-of-fact; but the handwriting, usually exceptionally clear and neat, is rough, smeared, and almost illegible on the one word *Oaksmith*, a classic Freudian revelation.[19]

V *Newspaper Publisher*

Between 1826 and 1829 Smith seems to have devoted himself to *belles lettres* but without public recognition or success. Three years after his marriage, he sold his interest in the *Argus* and in the fall of 1829[20] established two papers of his own: a weekly called the *Family Reader* and the daily *Portland Courier*. The *Family Reader*, conceived as a vehicle for both Seba's and Elizabeth's talents, was an ambitious, all-purpose journal which Smith described as "a useful, interesting, family miscellany with no political prejudice or vilification, with a condensed summary of world news and current literature, and hints on agriculture."[21] It was the *Portland Courier*, however, which brought Smith's work to national attention; for, during the paper's first winter, he introduced in its pages Jack Downing of Downingville, who was to become the most popular literary character of the age.

CHAPTER 2

Yankee Doodle

WHEN Seba Smith began publication of the *Portland Courier* in October, 1829, he proudly announced it as the first daily north and east of Boston and as a nonpartisan, independent venture. Earlier, with the *Eastern Argus*, the young Smith had engaged in journalistic and party rivalries. In 1824 he was involved in the threat of a duel, in an embarrassing physical encounter, and in some months of rancorous newspaper debate.[1] Although the two following court cases were decided in his favor, his commitment to conduct his paper with dignity and to avoid unedifying party strife was grounded in experience as well as in philosophy.

I *Jack Downing Appears on the Scene*

On January 1, 1830, the Maine legislature met in Portland. The preceding fall campaign, in Smith's assessment, had been carried on with bitterness and personal attacks unprecedented in the state. As the legislature opened, the two parties, the Democratic Republicans (supporting Andrew Jackson) and the National Republicans were so evenly balanced and each party was so intent on gaining control that for six weeks a series of tie votes and disputed ballots prevented the legislature from organizing itself. As the public business went undone, each party press set about discrediting its opposition. Only after two weeks and fifty ballots did the Maine senate manage to elect its presiding officer. Chosen was Joshua Hall, a politically inexperienced Methodist minister of the Democratic Republican persuasion; and he was elected, to the dismay of his own party, by National Republican votes.[2]

For three weeks Smith reported the sessions objectively but with increasing disapproval of the members' paralyzing partisanship. Then, as he described his inspiration thirty years later, he conceived the idea of satirizing state politics from the uncomprehending point of view of an ignorant country boy: "The author of these papers,

24

wishing to show the ridiculous position of the legislature in its true light, and also, by something out of the common track of newspaper writing, to give increased interest and popularity to his little daily paper, bethought himself of the plan to bring a green unsophisticated lad from the country into town . . . and . . . let him blunder into the halls of the legislature, and after witnessing for some days their strange doings, sit down and write an account of them to his friends at home in his own plain language."[3]

Among Smith's possible models for Downing and his letters, Mary Alice Wyman offers the rustic political letters of the fictional Vermonter Joe Strickland that were authored by George W. Arnold. A country boy in New York, Joe wrote home to his kinfolk his observations of the Albany legislature during the mid-1820's. Since Smith's reading at Bowdoin had included the classics of English and world literature, we may speculate that this inspiration went beyond the local and contemporary to examples of epistolary humor and satire like Tobias Smollett's *Humphry Clinker*, Oliver Goldsmith's *Citizen of the World* and the *Junius Letters*; but Jack Downing may also owe elements of his comic character to Don Quixote and Falstaff. Contemporary reviews of the Downing letters and details of the illustrations reinforce these possibilities by indicating that Smith's readers and illustrator saw his work as belonging to an old literary tradition.[4]

For the following three years, Seba Smith worked with the vernacular language and rural values; and he experimented with adventures, settings, and the culture of folk humor to create a folk perspective on the larger world. His own experience and his imagination filled out a form already existing in the mythology of American anecdote, song, and jokelore. At the end of three years, he published a book; in thirty years, a second; and between these two, he published three other volumes in which he experimented with the use of the culture of folk humor and with the presentation of the forms and figures of New England folk culture. Half a dozen volumes of spurious and pirated letters in numerous editions paid tribute to the vitality and national popularity of his character, Jack Downing.[5]

II *The Vernacular Perspective*

Smith's basic form was the mock letter that was suitable in its brevity for continued reappearance in a newspaper. That Jack

Downing appears in letters is of great esthetic importance. A letter being neither dialogue nor omniscient exposition, Jack's dialect, spelling, judgments, interpretations, and self-image appear concretely before the reader. As a form, Elizabeth Hardwick observes, the letter is always its writer's "own evidence, deposition, a self-serving testimony."[6] As he wrote, Seba Smith manipulated with increasing skill the potential of the letter form to present broad, comic incongruities in the official culture and to reveal subtler elements of incapacity and self-deceit in Jack Downing's character.

Jack's assessment of events implies his values, and his language creates the tone and delimits the universe of his folk culture. The point of view is essentially what Henry Nash Smith calls the "vernacular perspective,"[7] which, as he defines it in *Mark Twain: The Development of a Writer*, designates a language, a set of values, and ethical and esthetic assumptions. Jack Downing's attitudes, however, are not hostile to the established culture; in fact, they are considerably less lawless, audacious, and irreverent than comparable perspectives embodied later in Mark Twain's Huck Finn and especially in George Washington Harris' Sut Lovingood.

Most of the letters are from Jack to his cousin Ephraim, to his Uncle Joshua, and later to the editor of the *Portland Courier*. Cousin Ephraim, Uncle Joshua, Cousin Nabby, and his mother write to Jack; and some members of the Downing family write to each other. A few extracts from newspapers contrast formal language to the vernacular. By these means Smith achieves several political viewpoints and some variety of external perspectives on Jack. From the first, Smith created Jack as a New England village boy who is ignorant and naive to the point of foolishness about the ways of the larger world; but, at the same time, he is in his fashion honest (as far as his ignorance will allow him to see) and innocent.

Jack's ignorance is dense; but his foolishness at the opening is earnest, mild, and low-keyed as he expresses himself in intimate letters home. His foolishness is not that of deprivation; it is partly that of a second culture, the folk culture, and partly that of the traditional foolishness of a primitive consciousness. Jack's closeness to the traditional fool is clear from time to time: early in the book he begs Uncle Joshua not to "say Jack's a fool" (86);[8] and elsewhere Jack writes "I've had *this ere cold* and one thing another, so bad, I didn't feel hardly smart enough to write" (125). By placing the terms before the reader, Smith signals us that Jack is something of a fool, "hardly smart enough to write." Thus Jack's ignorance and innocence are complex.

For all Smith's own roots in down East folk culture, and for all his affection toward it, he felt sharply his own separation. In Boston in 1833, when the popularity of his creation was very high, Smith was introduced as Major Downing to Henry Clay. He wrote his wife that this made him feel very "awkward."[9] At other times the pastoral innocence and purity of his literary figure so beguiles Smith that Jack veers toward the sentimental version of pastoral. The pastoral implications of the goodness and the innocence that cluster around country life were so strong for the Smiths that Seba and Elizabeth at least once considered withdrawing to the forests of Maine to rear their boys. Here, "you shall be Adam and I shall be Eve, a little antique, perhaps," Elizabeth urged ingenuously.[10] But, Seba, having escaped from all that, declined.

Jack is no American Adam, no "figure of heroic innocence and vast potentialities, poised at the start of a new history."[11] Rather, he exists in complex tensions that include those between eighteenth-century sentimental and comic versions of pastoral. These tensions do much to separate Jack from the clichés of preceding Yankee bumpkins. But the general theme of Seba Smith's creation is conservative in the Age of Jackson: he holds before his audience the common man, who, for all his worth, is a creature of low intellectual and moral development.

III *Jack's Character Is Established*

The first letter of January 18, 1830, to "Cousin Ephraim Downing up in Downingville," presents Jack as a simple farm boy who has gone to town to sell the products of family industry: "When I come down to Portland I didn't think o' staying more than three or four days, if I could sell my load of ax handles, and mother's cheese, and cousin Nabby's bundle of footings" (42). Aunt Sally insists he remain to see Uncle Nat, who has "gone a freighting down to Quoddy" (42). While waiting, Jack goes to church in town, visits a museum, and "both Legislaters, the one they call the House and the one they call the Sinnet" (42). The letter relates that Jack's lazy Uncle Joshua, who is "Always reading newspapers and disputing politics" (42), had had an election bet with the postmaster, and that Jack must write to report he has lost.

Unaccustomed idleness gives Jack opportunity to gawk at the
political activity with Yankee Doodle simplicity. Reporting the
struggle over seating delegates, Jack takes the term "seat" literally:

> They kept disputing most all the time the two first days about a poor Mr.
> Roberts from Waterborough. Some said he shouldn't have a seat.
> . . . Others said . . . he was elected as fairly as any of 'em. —And Mr.
> Roberts himself said he was, and said he could bring men that would swear
> to it, and good men too. But notwithstanding all this, when they came to
> vote, they got three or four majority that he should n't have a seat. And I
> thought it a needless piece of cruelty, for they want crowded, and there was
> a number of seats empty. (43)

Smith intends less to comment on the delegate from Waterborough
than to satirize partisanship. But from this first letter, the comic presentation opens possibilities of a variety of meanings. Mr. Roberts'
colleagues are willing to dismiss his election; he and many "good
men" are willing to swear he was properly elected; and Jack is
puzzled—because he believes in the power of oaths.

    In the next vote, Roberts' opponent, Mr. Fowler, is seated. Jack
tries to account for the increased kindness: "They all declared there
was no party politics about it, and I dont think there was; for I noticed that all who voted that Mr. Roberts *should* have a seat, voted
that Mr. Fowler should not; and all who voted that Mr. Roberts
should *not* have a seat, voted that Mr. Fowler *should*. So, as they all
voted *both* ways, they must have acted as their consciences told
them, and I dont see how there could be any party about it" (44).
Jack's analysis not only displays his lumpkin reasoning but also
allows the reader to laugh at the simplicity of his faith in the honesty of politicians.

    A more sympathetic element of Jack's character, his generosity,
also leads him to misjudge events. Failure to seat Mr. Roberts seems
to him "needless cruelty." He entertains the possibility that partisanship might have seated Mr. Fowler but rejects it not only
because he reasons badly but also because he is not willing to infer
selfishness from the concrete human actions he sees. Before aban-
doning the elections, Seba Smith repeats the theme of Jack's
kindliness:

> It's a pity they could n't be allowed to have two speakers, for they
> seemed to be very anxious to choose Mr. Ruggles and Mr. Goodenow. They
> two had every vote, except one, and if they had had *that*, I believe they

would both have been chosen; as it was, however, they both came within a
humbird's eye of it. Whether it was Mr. Ruggles that voted for Mr.
Goodenow, or Mr. Goodenow for Mr. Ruggles, I can't exactly tell; but I
rather guess it was Mr. Ruggles voted for Mr. Goodenow, for he appeared
to be very glad that Mr. Goodenow was elected, and went up to him soon
after Mr. Goodenow took the chair, and shook hands with him as good-
natured as could be. I would have given half my load of ax handles, if they
could both have been elected and set up there together, they would have
been so happy. (44)

Jack's generosity, his good-natured delight in seeing people happy,
his unwillingness to impute selfish motives, his logic that allows one
vote to serve two, his belief in oaths and consciences are all,
ironically, part of his political incapacity. Smith's affection for
village talk and ways, as well as for political satire, is present in the
passage.

The second letter, one addressed to his political Uncle Joshua,
makes mild comedy of Jack's misconception that the Speaker of the
House is the one who most often speaks. Jack then attempts to
assess the significance of an organizational dispute:

O dear, uncle Joshua, these Legislaters have got the State into a dreadful
pickle. I've been reading the Portland Argus and the Portland Advertiser,
and it's enough to scare a Bunker Hill sojer out of his seven senses, to see
what we are all coming to. According to these papers, there are two very
clever parties in the State, that are trying with all their might to save us
from ruin. They are called *democratic republikins* and *national republikins;*
and you'd be perfectly astonished to see how hard they've worked, as these
papers say, in both Legislaters, to set things right, and get business a going
on well, so that we can have a governor, and live in peace and harmony,
and not break out into civil war, and all be ruined in a bunch. But it's
doubtful if they'll make out to save us after all; for there is such a set of
Jacksonites and Huntonites, that are all the time a plotting to bring us to
destruction, that I tell ye what 'tis, if something isn't done pretty soon, it'll
be gone goose with us. (48)

Partisan newspapers stir Jack's fear of civil turmoil and victimize
him with labels. The national titles of the two parties present
themselves to him as images of responsibility and harmony; but the
names of the local factions of the same two parties, presented dis-
paragingly by the newspapers, become images of threat and
destruction.

These first two letters establish Smith's basic construction of

Jack's character. Partly he is a vehicle for political satire. Partly he is
an engaging pastoral figure. The pastoral tradition, as Leo Marx
observes, developed a renewed and "peculiar credibility" in
America's early national period.[12] But Jack's good will and innocence, which are pleasing in themselves, often issue as political
incapacity. Three years later, when Smith put his book together, he
altered the newspaper sequence, omitted a number of letters, and
occasionally revised the language. The following discussion maintains the order of the book.

When Cousin Nabby writes the third letter to urge Jack home in
affectionately quarrelsome terms, Smith increases his number of
characters and defines Jack's personality from a new viewpoint.
Letter IV Smith did not write but chose to reprint from the Boston
Daily Advertiser because, as his headnote observes, this anonymous
work was in the "pure style" of the Downing family and was apparently the first of a flood of imitation Downing letters. In it, Uncle Joshua writes Jack from Boston to give an account of his travels:

> After seeing your letter to Ephraim as I said before, I concluded it
> wouldn't be a bad scheme to tackle up and take a load of turkies, some
> apple-sauce, and other notions that the neighbors wanted to get to market,
> and as your uncle Nat would be in Boston with the ax handles, we all
> thought best to try our luck there. Nothing happened worth mentioning on
> the road, nor till next morning after I got here. . . . I then got off my
> watch pretty curiously, as you shall be informed. I was down in the bar
> room, and tho't it well enough to look pretty considerable smart, and now
> and then compared my watch with the clock in the bar, and found it as near
> right as ever it was—when a feller stept up to me and ask'd how I'd trade?
> and says I, for what? and says he, for your watch—and says I, any way that
> will be a fair shake—upon that says he, I'll give you *my* watch and five
> dollars.—Says I, its done! He gave me the five dollars, and I gave him my
> watch. Now, says I, give me *your* watch—and, says he, with a loud laugh, I
> han't got none—and that kind aturn'd the laugh on me. Thinks I, let them
> laugh that lose. Soon as the laugh was well over, the feller thought he'd try
> the watch to his ear—why, says he, it dont go—no, says I, not without its
> carried—then I began to laugh—he tried to open it and couldn't start it a
> hair, and broke his thumb nail into the bargain. Won't she open, says he?
> Not's I know on, says I—and then the laugh seemed to take another turn.
> (51 - 52)

Constance Rourke, in her brilliant *American Humor*, mistakenly attributes the traditional trickster-tricked tale[13] to Jack rather than to
Uncle Joshua, but Seba Smith was not creating Jack as a hard

Yankee sharper. Neither the deceit of the trade nor the staccato style expresses Smith's slow, clear, affectionately ironic tone.

Samuel L. Clemens and W. D. Howells included the sketch in *Mark Twain's Library of Humor* (1888). Wide reprinting of this work not written by Smith suggests how the stereotype of the sharptrading Yankee of folk tradition constantly overspread the ingenuous character of Seba Smith's Jack. Smith's inclusion of the anecdote indicates how amusing he himself found the trickster figure, but his editorial headnote declares his unwillingness to let it represent Uncle Joshua.

IV Antiauthoritarian Themes

The next theme that Smith develops is Jack's reponse to authority, a basic comic theme that in this instance arises out of the political struggle following the death of Maine's Governor Enoch Lincoln. Law provided that in such an event the president of the senate should serve as acting governor. But, once a presiding officer was elected, his party, the Democratic Republicans, was unwilling, for fear of losing control of the senate, to let him serve. Meanwhile, the presiding officer of the past senate continued to serve as acting governor; but he expressed doubt that he was, in fact, legally governor of the state.

Jack observed the appearance of two possible governors and no certain governor with mingled uneasiness and exhilaration. The Lilliputian squabble opened to Jack the prospect of the collapse of order in his world: "Only think," he wrote, "no Governor, and no laws, but every body do jest as they're a mind to" (64). For Jack, the disappearance of law evokes a fantasy of release: he will hurry home to thrash his enemy Bill Johnson who had once called him a mean puppy and a coward. His fantasy hints at dreams of freedom to act out one's impulses. The upsurge of joy and aggressive power at the prospect of authority's disappearance is an ancient theme in the folk culture that was once institutionalized in the Saturnalia and the Feast of Fools and is still present in Mardi Gras celebrations. But ritual expressions of violent freedom survived in nineteenth-century New England in the folk culture only in reduced form in such occasions as militia musters and symbolically in jokes, comic legends, puppet shows, and the like.

This widespread antiauthoritarian theme seems to be one dimension of the human personality's drive toward wholeness of realization. Every society, apparently, creates myths which attack social and religious customs. We believe, as Matthew Hodgart says, that law and religion preserve our social structure; but we simultaneously feel at times that law and religion are intolerably restrictive.[14] The comic folk imagination always revels in subversion of restraint. The traces that primitive demonic subverters leave in carnival customs and in folklore are sometimes shadowy and disguised; and such demonism is a most muted, most minor facet of Smith's Jack Downing when he is compared to George Washington Harris' wild Sut Lovingood. But still, Smith's mild implication here is that common folk like Jack are restive; and they must, to some degree, live compulsively their more brutal impulses.

For his next letter, Smith continued the theme of the ordinary folk's delight in chaos and extended it to include an understated pleasure in open mockery of authority. As Jack wrote, the presiding officer, Joshua Hall, declared the senate adjourned; but the opposition party members, the National Republicans, kept their seats and talked of reorganizing. Elder Hall, afraid that his place might be taken, also kept his seat; but he repeatedly declared the senate adjourned:

The room was chock full of folks looking on, and the President told 'em the Sinnet was journed and they might as well go out, but they did not seem to keer tu, and they put their hats on and began to laugh like fun. The President sot still in his cheer, for I spose he thought if he left it, some of them are roguish fellers would be gettin into it. The man that keeps order, told the folks they must take their hats off when they were in the Sinnet; but they said they wouldn't, cause the Sinnet was ajourned. Then the man went and asked the President if the Sinnet was all ajourned, and the President said 'twas, and there was no doubt about it. And the folks felt so tickled to think they could wear their hats when the Sinneters were setting round the great table, that they kind of whistled a little bit all over the room. (75)

The low sound of pleasure susurrating through the crowd of ordinary citizens standing with their hats on in the presence of the senators creates an effectively understated image of defiance. It implies how ever-present to the people was their sense of restraint in the presence of authority. Form always has meaning, and the formality of the existing official world implies that its values are stable and indispensable to life. The spirit of folk humor denies officialdom's implied superiority and perfection. The folk devotion to official order is qualified in several ways: the villagers perceive faults in the official world, are annoyed by its pretentions, and are beguiled by a yearning for freedom.[15]

Two months later Smith returned to the theme from a third perspective: Jack's vision of himself as the figure of authority. Jack writes his Uncle Joshua in intimate confidence that he might be nominated for governor: "Think of that, uncle; your poor neffu Jack, that last summer was hoeing about among the potatoes, and chopping wood, and making stone walls, like enough before another summer comes about, will be Governor of the State. I shall have a better chance to flog Bill Johnson then, than I should last winter, if we had n't had no Governor nor no laws; for I spose a Governor has a right to flog any body he's a mind to" (86).

Jack's extravagant assessment of his chances comically dramatizes how feeble his grasp of reality is. Furthermore, by returning to this theme when Jack imagines himself as governor, Smith modifies our pleasure in Jack's freedom, simplicity, and directness. His loose fantasy of himself as a governor who is above the law presents the common man as inferior to the gentleman in self-control. Jack's simple aggressiveness, like his simple good will, presents an infantile, undifferentiated consciousness. But, at the same time, Jack's fantasy is true to the folk conviction that the great are indeed above the power of the law and have privileges of conduct that the poor can only dream of. One of the common folk themes is that the majesty and justice of the law is a fiction; that power, not justice, orders society. In the high culture this theme is frequently expressed in the ambiguity of comedy. "It is not right," says the mad Don Quixote when he frees the criminals, "that honorable men should serve as executioners of their fellows. . . ."

In a meditation about the strict order in bandit societies and in armies, Miguel de Unamuno argues that "it can be said of all types of human justice that they sprang from injustice, from the need injustice had to sustain and perpetuate itself. Justice and order came into the world to maintain violence and disorder."[16] Jack's absurd, oafish attitude toward authority, therefore, is less simple than it seems. Seba Smith's continuing examination of official culture from the point of view of folk culture, as that culture is embodied in Jack Downing, generates (sometimes without Smith's intention) judgments of the established culture as well as feelings of condescension toward the common man. Still, understated, and to a degree ambiguous as it is, this natural rebelliousness of the masses threatened, to conservatives like Seba Smith, the collapse of the social order.

V Folk Humor

Research in folklore and literature is just beginning to provide formal categories and to interpret the motives and functions of folk humor. Although conclusions await comprehensive collections, Mikhail Bakhtin's recent study of Rabelais' world offers concepts of the nature and function of traditional European folk humor which are applicable to a great deal of nineteenth-century, American popular and folk humor. After establishing the categories of medieval French folk humor, Bakhtin argues that these comic forms present "a completely different, nonofficial, extraecclesiastical and extrapolitical aspect of the world, of man, and of human relations; they build a second world and a second life outside officialdom. . . ."[17] The function of folk humor, in Rabelais' world, is to celebrate a "temporary liberation from the prevailing truth and from the established order." It expresses joy, high spirits; it is hostile to all that is ready-made and completed, "to all pretense at immutability. . . ." Instead, folk laughter sees the world in "gay relativity." Finally, this folk laughter is ambivalent: "it is gay, triumphant, and at the same time mocking, deriding." The purpose of its destructive element, as Bakhtin sees it, its principle of degradation, is to materialize—to bring officials and institutions down to earth so that something better may be brought forth.[18]

Bakhtin's theory of a hopeful and fruitful aim seems an effort to dignify and defend the destructive element in folk humor. Its delight in destruction may, however, be seen simply as a dark or evil human impulse that is given high-spirited expression. C. G. Jung sees wildness, wantonness, and irresponsibility as elements of the primitive consciousness, of "an absolutely undifferentiated human consciousness, corresponding to a psyche that has hardly left the animal level."[19] But whatever its ultimate aim, one of the basic motives of folk humor, as manifested, say, in the joke, is to destroy—as well as to bring down to earth mere idealistic and spiritual pretense. Another of its basic motives is to celebrate the joy in freedom from restraint, to express a yearning for the Golden Age of primitive innocence when man could express his impulses without thought or shame. Politics aside, Jack's wish that everybody could be happily seated and his ingenuously expressed desire for power and triumph were strong subliminal forces contributing to the enormous popular success of the Downing figure.

VI *Burlesque Forms*

Jack's ambition to be governor pleases his political Uncle Joshua. Satirizing America's opening political system, Smith has Uncle Joshua reveal to Jack that even an unsuccessful candidate can expect an appointment to an office. To exploit the appeal of honorifics, Uncle Joshua suggests that Jack campaign under a party name that combines the titles of both national organizations. Finally, he proposes that a series of meetings be held throughout the state and that each one be reported in the newspapers. To illustrate his meanings, the shrewd, conscienceless, practical Uncle Joshua sends samples of contrived reports and resolutions—documents which Smith creates as burlesques. In content, these satirize exploitation of patriotism, flattery of the public, and crisis-mongering; as literary types, they ridicule a variety of rhetorical forms.

Nineteenth-century American popular and folk humor are rich in examples of burlesque sermons, prayers, and religious tracts; literary burlesques (such as those by Mark Twain, Bret Harte, and others); burlesques of political speeches, caucuses, and legislative sessions; and burlesque autobiographies and biographes. Behind these lay a well-developed European tradition, strong since medieval times, when parody of sacred forms was particularly popular: written examples exist of the Liturgy of Drunkards; the Liturgy of the Gamblers; parodies of the Gospels, of prayers, hymns, psalms, and others. For secular literature, artists produced parodies of debates, dialogues, epics, and orations; Erasmus' *Praise of Folly* is an eminent example.

In eighteenth-century England, literary burlesques became a fashionable part of high culture as works by Jonathan Swift, John Gay, and Lady Mary Wortley Montagu testify. In the folk culture, marketplace shows of England and France continued their ancient clownish mockery of the high-born, the fashionable, and the types of military, ecclesiastical, and governmental authority figures. The fact that political burlesques were as abundant in nineteenth-century America as religious parodies were in fifteenth-century France may hint that politics had become America's true religion. The broad function of burlesque forms, Mikhail Bakhtin argues, is

to express hostility to the established forms that imply that they are
permanent, that they preserve order and justice. Burlesques mock
the imperfections of such existing forms; unmask their immoralities,
their hidden uses to their supporters; and imply their imper-
manence.

The comic mode is complex. On the surface, Smith mocks Jacksonian democracy; but, by burlesquing the traditional forms, he unconsciously opens to doubt the value and stability of those institutions which, as a professed conservative, he wished to preserve.

VII   *The Downings Learn the Lessons of Jacksonian Politics*

After Uncle Joshua's letter and Jack's reply, a burlesque
newspaper account of the "Grand Caucus at Downingville" follows;
and it is subheaded, between dramatically pointing fingers, "THE
LONG AGONY OVER." News for the report, the *Courier* wrote,
was carried by Captain Jehu Downing, who, after his horse fell and
broke its rider's arm and ribs, was attended by Dr. Zachariah Downing. Thereupon the express was forwarded by Lieutenant Timothy
Downing, who ran down three horses. The meeting, the *Courier*
reported, was called to order by "the venerable and silver-haired
patriarch, old Mr. Zebedee Downing," who presided over the election of Joshua Downing, Esquire, as chairman, and Mr. Ephraim
Downing as secretary. Mr. Jacob Downing moved appointment of a
resolutions committee consisting of Jotham Downing, Ichabod
Downing, Zenas Downing, Levi Downing, and Isaiah Downing.

The committee reported: "Resolved, conditionally, that in case
General Jackson should be likely to be re-elected, we highly and
cordially approve of his administration, and believe him to be second to none but Washington; but in case he should stand no chance
of re-election, we resolve him to be the ignorant tool of a corrupt
faction, plotting to destroy the liberties of the country" (98). The
report concludes with burlesques of private documents—two
quarrelsome family letters to Jack that harshly demand the offices
of sheriff and land agent.

The comic series of Biblical first names, all Downings, ingenuously exposes the Grand Caucus as a family conspiracy; but the private
letters reveal that the clan's unity is for appearance only. The
resolution is devoid of any issues, information, or principle but that
of expediency. Specifically, Smith satirizes the pursuit of offices in

state and local politics through nepotism. Two months later Jack writes that he has lost the election. "However, worst come to worst, I know what I can do," he confides to Uncle Joshua. "If Judge Smith's got in . . . I'll see if I cant work it so as to get an office under him.—You see I kept pretty still along for some time before election, and I guess I can manage it so as to make him think I lectioneered for him" (100 - 1). Jack's half-year devotion to state politics has led him to deceit. He sees the advantages for himself of shrewd closeness about his actions and intent.

During the election, Jack observes a man busily carrying voters to the polls. When Jack asks for whom they are voting, "Why, says he, they vote for whichever goes arter em, you goose-head you. Ah, says I, is that the way they work it? And where do they bring 'em from? O, says he, down round the wharves, and the outskirts of the town and any where that they can catch 'em. Well, well, thinks I to myself, I've got a new rinkle, I see how this business is done now. So off I steered and hired a horse and wagon . . . " (102).

Jack did not learn quite enough, however, for none of the fifty men that he carried to the polls voted for him. As Mark Twain observed later, a successful fraud is not comic. But Uncle Joshua reports better news of the Downingville vote: for the Honorable Samuel E. Smith, none; for the Honorable Jonathan G. Hunton (probably Seba Smith's candidate), none; for the Honorable JACK DOWNING, 87. From Smith's conservatively critical point of view, the Downings are learning step by step the lessons of Jacksonian politics: any man may pursue public office; party solidarity brings control; issues should be avoided as divisive; the vote of the riffraff can assure party victory.

Broadly, Jack's trip to town has brought about his fall from virtue. His good will does not disappear; his high spirits increase as he becomes aware of more possibilities in his life; but his ambition begets deceit. He learns to mask the truth about his actions to get himself an office, but he has neither the intelligence nor the moral impulse to consider the consequences of his acts. The possibility of buying votes makes him think, "well, well." He sees in high office only the excitement of fighting, the pleasures of vengeance and laziness.

The evil that the common man brings to politics, as Smith sees it, is not dramatic but banal. Such a man's innocent selfishness encompasses no desire to harm others, but such a man has no moral or intellectual capacity to lead. In fact, Jack's conduct is guided by the common man's virtues: confidence nurtured in a limited society, ambition, and the tradition of family solidarity. Smith's belief in government by the propertied and educated implied that civilization is complex and is maintained by effort and intelligence. The country Jack he creates is incapable of seeing any complexities in his world and is equally incapable of effort.

VIII   Jack's American Language

Whatever the readers' response to Smith's political uses of Jack, they were delighted with him as a fictional creation. In fact, John Neal told Mrs. Smith in 1833 that: "Major Downing is the subject of conversation in all the steamboats, stages, and taverns along the road."[20] No small part of the public's interest and pleasure in Jack must have come from Smith's device of having him write home to the folks "in his own plain language."

Except for the stage, where comic Yankees had been popular since Royall Tyler's *The Contrast* (1787), Smith's was the first literary attempt to capture the qualities of the New England vernacular, and it was an immediate popular success. There is nothing exaggerated or strained in Jack's language. It never approaches caricature, nor does Smith let a passion for phonetic accuracy stand in the way of intelligibility. The down East dialect is, in fact, very similar in its essentials to the ordinary vulgar American speech of other early-settled areas such as the Appalachian hills. H. L. Mencken argues that, although James Russell Lowell set forth seven peculiarities of Yankee speech in his preface to the *Biglow Papers*, First Series, the only true distinction is in the pronunciation of some *a* sounds, a pronunciation not to be captured by our inadequate system of English spelling.[21]

According to the Federal Writers' Project guide to Maine, the common speech, like that of the Carolina and Kentucky mountaineers, is still that of the original English-Scottish-Irish stock. This language retains many old grammatical forms and pronunciations, and some of the vocabulary harks back to Elizabethan times. The spoken quality of Maine speech, the guide book insists, is impossible to capture in print because its peculiarities lie in subtleties of enunciation, "a nasal quality . . . with a hesitancy in delivery."[22] Smith had a keen ear, and the good sense to content himself with the flavor of down East talk without excessive attention to such details of enunciation and delivery. The result was a literary creation which was easily readable yet had an air of perfect authenticity to native speakers of the same rural New England dialect. Indeed, Ralph Waldo Emerson says that old Ezra Ripley could never be persuaded that Jack Downing was not a real person.[23]

Smith's experiment with dialect writing had far-reaching literary consequences, as Mencken indicates in his study of the development of American English. In the age's controversy over the propriety of Americanisms, neither scholars like Noah Webster and Timothy Dwight nor literary rebels like James Kirk Paulding and Walt Whitman succeeded in changing American literary English. Lowly newspaper humorists, beginning with Seba Smith and his imitators and culminating with Mark Twain, deserve the credit for "laying the foundations for a genuinely colloquial and national style of writing."[24]

Ernest Hemingway's often-quoted judgment that all American literature comes from *Huckleberry Finn* is based on his admiration for Mark Twain's use of the American vernacular as a literary vehicle. It has been demonstrated that Mark Twain derived this technique, which he used with the skill of a great artist, from the newspaper tradition of American dialect humor. Particularly clear are his connections with the humorists of the Old Southwest, but less often noted is the influence of Seba Smith on these writers, such as William Tappan Thompson.[25] Thus, though it would obviously be absurd to assert that all American literature comes from Seba Smith, the colloquial style used so effectively by Mark Twain, by Hemingway, William Faulkner, John Steinbeck, Langston Hughes, Richard Wright, J. D. Salinger, and others was first successfully achieved in the Jack Downing letters.

CHAPTER 3

Yankee Doodle Dandy

J ACK'S ambition and foolish incapacity soon lead him to enter national politics. To Uncle Joshua he writes, "I am tired of hard work, and I mean to have an office some how or other yet" (104). Innocent of doubts about his competence, he plans to run for Congress; and to get to Washington, he connives to have Uncle Joshua present him as a tariff man. "I was agoin to take sides against the tariff so as to please Gineral Jackson and all his party," he writes. "You know they've been mad enough with the tariff to eat it up. But the Portland Advertiser has been blowin away lately and praising up the tariff and telling what a fine thing tis, and fact, *it* has brought the old gineral round" (104). Jack's home-boy assumption that Portland editorials have changed President Andrew Jackson's mind is Smith's thrust at the self-importance of reporters. At the national level, Smith is satirizing the inconsistency and the political motivation of Jacksonian tariff policies.

I *National Ambitions and Country Virtues*

As Seba Smith moved his own attention and his literary creation from local to national politics, his objects of attack grew increasingly specific: the Jacksonian "spoils system," the national party's pursuit of contributions and of getting out the vote, its emphasis on winning, its disregard for ideological matters, its avoidance of issues, and its cult of personality.[1] But, as Smith became more self-conscious in his aim to enlighten and reform, some of the letters become trite. His last one for 1830, from young Sarah in Portland to Cousin Nabby in the country, praises in the pastoral vein, the superiority of rural life. Scorning the "Portland beaux," she praises her country neighbor, Sam Josslyn: "He is educated enough to know the age of his cows and oxen, to know how to cultivate a field of corn or a patch of potatoes; can read his bible, and say the ten commandments, and what is better, Sam can *keep* them all" (105).

40

She attributes her Uncle Joshua's "success" (he is usually an idle figure) to "good management, economy in his dress and frugality in his living" (105). The ideal woman must be "capable, neat, industrious, and amiable." But in the city, she observes, such characteristics are disregarded. "No, indeed, my dear," she writes in the prissy superiority of complacent provincialism, the city girl "must have a smattering of French, must be able to drum the music out of the piano, to sing and dance, or all in one word, she must be *genteel*" (106). All Sarah's virtues are coarsely self-serving and prudential. Her scorn of music, French, and dancing in the city is expressed with parochial smugness. Like Charles Dickens' Gradgrind, Sarah sees the ideal life as utilitarian and narrow.

The trite vocabulary and the genteel style open the possibility that Smith is satirizing Sarah's philosophy. And, in fact, Jack's following letter to Uncle Joshua complains that Sally's education is making her so "vain and accomplished" that she has taken to calling herself Sarah. The entire letter, however, indicates that Smith was momentarily carried away by the rhetoric of his copybook virtues and that he had his second thoughts later. He did not reprint Sarah's letter in his 1859 volume.

II *A Tax on Old Bachelors*

Jack's report of the 1831 legislature began early in February. As the Huntonites had controlled it the previous year, the Jacksonites, or Democratic Republicans, now did so. The first letters again satirize perturbations over partisan issues. The letter reporting adjournment of the 1831 session includes an account of a burlesque law introduced by one high-spirited Mr. Shapleigh, who proposed a committee to consider an annual tax on old bachelors "to be appropriated for the use and support of a certain class of ladies usually known by the name of Old Maids" (129). A motion to table the proposal was rejected, but some sober member finally urged his colleagues to reflect before they committed an impropriety; thereupon the order was indefinitely postponed. This burlesquing of one's official self and function is comparable to the burlesquing that priests, deacons, and choir-children celebrated in twelfth-century Europe at the Feast of Fools.[2] The tradition of burlesque laws, burlesque debate, and burlesque functions during the closing sessions of state legislatures survives today.[3]

These events stimulated Jack to poetry, which he included in the letter. Not exactly appropriate to Jack's character, the poem is a comic dream-vision of the old bachelors' refusing to pay the tax and consequently being sold at public auction for their debt. Old maids buy them, and each triumphantly carries home a man. Constructed of clichés, the thumping doggerel maintained by auxiliaries and articles, the verse has grotesque comic vigor.

III   *Jack Goes to Washington*

President Jackson's problems with his Cabinet and his involvement in the Peggy Eaton affair, a much publicized social feud in the period 1830 - 31, offered fine possibilities for Smith's satire. The Cabinet was split between supporters of John C. Calhoun and those of Martin Van Buren as successors to the President; and, when Jackson attempted to compel social recognition of a former barmaid who had married Secretary of War John H. Eaton, her status became a political issue. Some Cabinet members' wives, including Calhoun's, refused to receive Mrs. Eaton. Dissension in the Cabinet culminated in the resignations of the Attorney General and the Secretaries of State, Navy, Treasury, and War. In this period of crisis, Smith was inspired to have Jack go to Washington and lend Jackson a hand.

Jack has heard that four of President Jackson's secretaries have resigned, leaving "the poor old General to do all the work alone. Why, uncle, the'd no more patriotism than your old hoss" (134), Jack wrote, innocently mixing his desire for salary with his desire to serve. Before setting out on foot, Jack got Cousin Sally to mend his trousers; and her letter about the incident provides a decent perspective on Jack. Ashamed of his ragged clothes, she wrote that his appearance "almost made my heart ache" (136). In an attempt to talk "a little common sense" into him, she urges him "to let politics alone, and go back to Downingville and take care of his farm and his poor infirm father and mother" (136)—surely Smith's moral judgment. But Jack ignores his responsibilities. As for his appearance, he believes all the President wants is "a good man, and one who has been firm in support of him" (137). While Jack is out of the house, Sally schemes to delay him; with Penelope-like ingenuity, she pulls out the thread from all the mending she has done. Always the creature of mindless action, Jack, when he sees no progress, decides to go ragged rather than wait. Although Sally recognizes that Jack deceives himself about his own integrity and high-mindedness, she finds no way to make him see himself.

Although ideas give Jack the "agitations," he is determined to "make something" of himself. As a comic figure, he is blind to the basic paradox of his character: ambition without capacity. In Seba Smith's conservative judgment, Jacksonian politics was awakening in common men the ambition to "rise" in the world; but it was doing so without educating them in the discipline, work, knowledge, and sense of responsibility that should accompany leadership. Jackson himself had said in his first annual message that "the duties of public officers are . . . so plain and simple that men of intelligence may readily qualify themselves for their performance."[4] Indeed, the party of Jackson, in its drive to get votes, Smith implies, did not merely give offices to incompetents; it contributed to a broad cultural decay, denied differences in competence, and encouraged the common man in his natural shiftlessness to accept himself as he found himself. Blind to his shortcomings, innocent of alternatives, Jack believes himself to be the measure of the world.

Jack's ambition, which is necessarily vague, is incongruously grandiose, largely materialistic, something to "make the common folks stare" (133). His imagination turns constantly on what the folks back in Portland will say when he becomes a "success." Jack imagines his achievement in coarse, childish terms: "You'll see me coming dressed up like a lawyer, with a fine carriage and three or four hosses. And then them are chaps in Portland that used to laugh at me so about being Governor, may sneeze at me if they dare to, and if they dont keep out of my way I'll ride right over 'em" (142). Elevate the common man, Smith implies, and he brings to his high seat an undisciplined ego, gross manners, and an insolent joy in his power. Deeply imbedded in folk culture lies the dark demonic.

In Jack's walk from Portland to Washington, he calls on various newspaper editors; but he is always comically innocent or ignorant (not separable categories in Jack's character) about their obvious party affiliations. When Smith creates a fictional encounter between Jack and the formidable anti-Jacksonian Mordeciah M. Noah, the real-life editor of the New York *Courier and Inquirer,* Noah catechizes Jack on Democratic Republican doctrine: "I told him I had always had some kind of an idea of it, "Jack wrote, "but I didn't know as I could explain it exactly" (143 - 44). When Noah tells Jack that the basic philosophic principle of the Democratic Republican party is either to stick to Andrew Jackson through thick and thin or

to face the ruin of the country (144) the cult of personality and
loyalty to men in power rather than to principles is the target of
Smith's satire.

Having Jack say that he knows his ideas but cannot express them
is Smith's neat satiric use of a common folk response which satirizes
Jack's loose thinking and his easy acceptance of his own ignorance.
Such culturally authorized adjustment to ignorance represents a
part of Jack's folk culture which, Smith felt, disqualified the common man for leadership. As Smith presented his views in the 1831
letters, to be unenlightened about one's self and one's motives and
abilities is not an absolutely negative condition, a condition of
deprivation. Jack positively seeks to maintain his comfortable
darkness. Smith puts the element of intention in Jack's ignorance so
delicately that it appears as really a prereflective apprehension of
consciousness. By choosing to listen to Uncle Joshua, by choosing
not to listen to Cousin Sally, and by saying he cannot explain his
political principles, Jack reveals the intentional element in his ignorance. Maintaining ignorance is a common human project, and to
open it to view provides a source of comic release.

IV   The Peggy Eaton Affair

In Washington, Jack at once intrudes in the Peggy Eaton affair.
By making Jack a participant, Smith satirizes its triviality, its
emotionalism, and its violence. Down East in Maine, Jack wrote, if
folks got ever so mad, "they didn't do nothing but talk and jaw one
another; but here if any body doesn't suit 'em, fact they'll up and
shoot him in a minute" (145). Seeing such violence in Washington,
Jack asks Uncle Joshua to send him his old fowling piece. Jack has
heard that "they come pretty near having a shooting scrape here
yesterday," something about Mr. Eaton's wife. The papers report
that Mr. Eaton has declared "he'd fight somebody, and he didn't
care who" (145). To Jack's down East horror, the parties are not going to box but to shoot at one another.

In the next letter, Smith creates a second satiric perspective on
the Eaton affair. Cousin Ephraim writes that General Combs (a
reference to the way President Jackson dressed his hair) has turned
Uncle Joshua out because Cousin Nabby, Mrs. Inkhorn, and Mrs.
Thimblebury, whose names are all echoic or anagrammatic, would
not invite Mrs. No-tea to their husking and quilting parties. The
reduction of the Eaton affair to a village social squabble has some

allegorical precision, but both the humor and the invention are labored. Smith rather baldly expresses his judgment that the affair was trivial, intensely personal, and irrationally violent.[5]

CHAPTER 4

In the Kitchen Cabinet

A FTER a persistent, ragged, poverty-stricken wait in Washington, Jack gets his reward: President Jackson calls on him for help. Thus satirically Smith implies the quality of Jackson's political advisors—an unofficial group of confidants called by his political opponents the "Kitchen Cabinet." The fictional encounter between the down East country boy and the President is realized with homely, comic vigor. Afire over the imprisonment of four Maine farmers by the British in the Madawaska boundary dispute, the President entrusts Jack not with an office but with a commission as a captain in the United States Army, gives him a pocket full of money, and orders him to fight the British and bring back the prisoners.

Enormously inflated, Jack writes his Uncle Joshua another fantasy about his riding into Downingville in his full regimentals to enjoy the chagrin of his former sweetheart. Jack swells with scorn for her new husband, once a schoolmaster, but now a farmer "hoeing potatoes for a living" (152). Nor does he forget to threaten the Portland boys who had laughed at his ambition. Not all the men are hot for war, but he raises his company and marches to Madawaska, only to find the "prisoners" already released.

I Soldier Jack

In his first military report, Captain Downing ingenuously reveals to President Jackson the reason for his disappointment at missing a war: "If I could only got down there a little sooner and fit sich a great battle as you did at New Orleans, my fortune would have been made for this world. I should have stood a good chance then to be President of the United States, one of these days. And that's as high as ever I should want to get" (160). Unfortunately for Jack's hopes, the British have treated the prisoners humanely; therefore he cannot make blood flow to advance his career. The influence of military glory on the spirit of the young nation Alexis de Tocqueville called "inconceivable." General Jackson, he said, twice elected to be their President by the Americans, "is a man of violent temper and very moderate talents; nothing in his whole career ever proved him qualified to govern a free people; and, indeed, the majority of the enlightened classes of the Union has always opposed him. But he was raised to the Presidency, and has been maintained there, solely by the recollection of a victory which he gained, twenty years ago, under the walls of New Orleans; a victory which was, however, a very ordinary achievement. . . ."[1]

Years later, in Seba Smith's satires about the Mexican War, he repeated this theme: common soldiers may die, but officers and political leaders tend to be passionately prowar, for their common secret ambition is at one stroke to establish a reputation and enter the ranks of the great—and war best provides this peculiar opportunity.

II *The "Ginneral's" Friend and Adviser*

After the collapse of his hopes to become an instant hero, Jack returns to Washington to have the first of his sessions with the President as his confidential friend and adviser. To the new Captain Downing, the President opens his heart about the difficulty of governing a country where "folks will act pretty much as they are a mind to" and where almost everybody wants "to have a finger in the pye" (178). In unbuttoned invective, Jackson denounces all opposition presidential candidates—Henry Clay, John C. Calhoun, and William Wirt—and says he himself would never have run for reelection except to assure the succession of Martin Van Buren. Seba Smith's comic presentation of Jackson, however, is always understated, sometimes affectionate, but never so gross and so unrestrained as the ones many newspapers of the time permitted.

In an account of Jack and the President drinking to Jackson's 1832 victory, Smith contrives a parody of the kinds of toasts that were exchanged at political dinners.[2] In Smith's burlesque, the drinks honor Jackson's unexpected Pennsylvania victory: "And now, says the President, I will give you a toast. The state of Pennsylvania, the most patriotic State in the Union; for though I go against all her great public interests, still she votes for me by an overwhelming majority" (187). Modern historians have recalled that Pennsylvanians favored the United States Bank, internal improvements, the protective tariff system, and opposed Van Buren yet voted for Jackson: a performance that Edward Pessen calls incredible.[3]

Smith's implication of Jackson's delighted astonishment at the voters' performance is broadly comic. Jack toasts Downingville as the "most unwavering democratic republican town in New England." "Good," said the President. "You shall have a Post Office established there" (187). To the President's toast to Martin Van Buren, Jack responds with "Uncle Joshua Downing, the most thorough going republican in Downingville." "Good," said the President, "I understand you, Captain Downing; your Uncle Joshua shall have the Post Office" (187). The little burlesque serves not only to degrade significant exchanges of political toasts but also to emphasize the triumphs of the Jacksonian personality cult over issues, the creation of unneeded offices, and, finally, the thematic charge that such offices are awarded merely on the basis of party loyalty.

III *The Nullification Controversy*

Jack's December 8, 1832, letter is Seba Smith's first comic analysis of the nullification controversy, a complex dispute which does not allow broad summary without some distortion. The standard interpretation has been that South Carolina cotton planters, suffering from declining prices and exhausted soil, could not compete with planters in the new Southwestern lands. Nor could the commercial center of the state, Charleston, compete with New York or even the new Southern cotton ports. Blaming their economic depression and their declining power on the tariffs, South Carolinians tried to nullify the tariffs of 1828 and 1832, defied President Jackson's attempts to enforce these laws, and thus "brought the nation to the verge of civil war."[4]

Calhoun, at this time Vice-President, was within days to be elected United States Senator from South Carolina. An ingenious proslavery constitutional theorist, he had affirmed and elaborated the doctrine of nullification—briefly, that single states could nullify federal laws. He was passionately ambitious to be president. However, he alone had not created the controversy, a many-faceted situation, nor was he its only leader.

In his letter Jack describes how Jackson appealed to him for help with a "delicate job":

There's that miserable ambitious Calhoun has been trying this dozen years to be President of the United States; but he can't make out, so now he is determined to lop off a few of the southern States and make himself President of them. But if he don't find himself mistaken my name isn't Andrew Jackson. As he said this he started up on his feet, and begun to march across the floor with a very soldier-like step, and his eyes fairly flashed fire. No, said he, Capt. Downing, he must wait till somebody else is President besides me before he can do that. Let him move an inch by force in this business, if he dares. I'll chase him as far beyond Tennessee as it is from here to there, but what I'll catch him and string him up by the neck to the first tree I can find. (188)

Smith's technique in the letter is that of the caricaturist: the pronullification forces in the South are personified in one figure, Calhoun, who is broadly sketched as an embodied passion to be president. His ambition is degraded by being presented as merely personal. Finally, the image of Calhoun is strikingly deflated with Jackson's scornful word, "miserable." The final fantasy of catching the wretched, fleeing, defeated creature and hanging him by the neck from the first tree releases a feeling of triumph in a tidy solution. At the same time, the passage maintains the thematic image of the intemperate Jackson.

In the following letter, Uncle Joshua writes Jack his reaction to the President's December 10 Proclamation to the People of South Carolina, which characterized nullification as "an impractical absurdity." Uncle Joshua is delighted, but he is annoyed that Squire Dudley, an old Federalist, is equally delighted and also wants to praise Jackson's stand. Next day the Downingville Jacksonians, with Uncle Joshua as chairman, call a public meeting to pass resolutions in favor of the Proclamation. But they shut the Federal party out of the public meeting; and, when the Federalists gather outside the window and begin to hurrah for Jackson, Uncle Joshua sends young Ephraim and Joel out with a piece of scythe to drive away his doctrinally impure fellow supporters of the act. While his picture is true to New England's enthusiastic response to Jackson's Proclamation, Smith is mostly bemused at the divisiveness of party and at Downingville's lack of dignity and sense.

What stimulated Seba Smith's comic invention were the excesses of South Carolinian rhetoric and action. For example, at one point in the controversy, Representative George McDuffie declared "The Union, such as the majority have made it, is a foul monster, which those who worship, after seeing its deformity, are worthy of their chains."[5] The South Carolina legislature gave Governor Robert Y. Hayne authority to create a military force by accepting volunteers and by draft of Carolinians between eighteen and forty-five (including Unionists), and authority to spend four-hundred thousand dollars for arms. Through late 1832 and into 1833 the passion of action and rhetoric continued to mount.[6]

The frenzy that troubled Seba Smith remains something of a puzzle today. The modern scholar who has most fully studied the elements of the crisis, William W. Freehling, concludes that there was indeed some hysteria in the movement. That a tariff, the meaning of passages of the Constitution, and questions of political theory should provoke such fury, in South Carolina particularly, indicates to Freehling and to Charles G. Sellers, Jr., that a complicated psychological torment over slavery lay at or near the center of the causal factors.[7]

South Carolina passion frightens the sometimes courgeous Jack. As usual, Smith's caricature arises from a concrete event. South Carolina congressman James Blair became so enraged at being called "Tory" by Duff Green, the editor of the *United States Telegraph,* that he assaulted Green with a club on the streets of Washington.[8] After this incident, Jack wrote Cousin Ephraim that he was "kind of wamble-cropt" about marching against the nullifiers after all:

If they've got many such fellers there as one Ginneral Blair there is here from that State, I'd sooner take my chance in the woods forty miles above Downingville, fighting bears and wolves and catamounts, than come within gunshot of one of these Carolina giants. He's a whaler of a feller, as big as any two men in Downingville. They say he weighs over three hundred pounds. About a week ago he met Ginneral Duff Green in the street and he fell afoul of him with a great club and knocked him down, and broke his arm and beat him almost to death, jest because he got mad at something Mr. Green said in his paper. And what makes me feel more skittish about getting into the hands of such chaps, is, because he says he couldn't help it. He says all his friends persuaded him not to meddle with Ginneral Green, and he tried as hard as he could to let him alone, but he "found himself unequal to the effort." So Green like to got killed (193).

The fiction ends with Blair, armed with four pistols, two dirks, and a great knife, shooting for no reason in a Washington theater at the players. When the audience tries to subdue him, he begins to "rave like a mad ox," and they all run. Jack concludes that he cannot fight such men as Blair.

To personify frenzy and fanaticism, Blair is an apt choice. Even Blair's fellow South Carolinian Thomas Grimké found Blair's

simultaneous devotion to the Union and to nullification to be con-
tradictory. Again Smith's technique is caricature: Blair's size and
weaponry are grotesquely exaggerated; his bluster is mocked and
degraded by Jack's fear; and to have Blair shoot at actors effectively
suggests madness in his violence. This scene suggests the possibility
that Smith was recalling Don Quixote's slashing with his sword at
the dolls in the puppet theater. The stroke of having Blair declare
himself uncontrollable because of what he read in the newspapers
caricatures the irrationality, as it seemed to Smith, in the nullifiers'
conduct.

Jack's letter of January 17, 1833, addressed to the editor of the
Portland Courier (a version of real Seba Smith) presents Jack in the
White House chatting with the President about his message to
Congress. In the spirit of folk wisdom, Jack responds to the
President's invitation for comment by offering an exemplum. He
recalls joining other boys to raft logs across Sebago Pond. During a
storm, Jack, Joel, Ephraim, and the village bully, Bill Johnson,
decide to cross by lashing their logs together. Shortly Bill complains
that his side is hardest to row, so one of the boys changes with him.
Then he frets to have his old place back. When the boys complain,
he responds with an ultimatum: if they do not change in five
minutes, he will cut the lashings and cross alone. "And before we
had hardly time to turn around, he declared the five minutes were
out, and up hatchet and cut the lashings, and away went Bill on his
own log, bobbing and rolling about, and dancing like a
monkey. . ." (196). Bill falls in the water, almost drowns, and ends
by begging the boys to take him and his log back into the raft,
which they do. "And now Gineral," Jack concludes, "this is jest
what I think: if you let South Carolina cut the lashings you'll see
such a log-rolling in this country as you never see yet. The old
Gineral started up and marched across the floor like a boy. Says he,
Major Downing, she sha'nt cut the lashings while my name is Andrew Jackson" (197).

The reduction of the ship-of-state metaphor to a log raft provides
a homely symbol of the Union, through which Jack for the first time
gives sensible advice. From such passages Jennette Tandy derives
her assessment that Jack is a "crackerbox philosopher," that he
represents the viewpoint of the common man, and that he appeals
to the "common sense" of his audience.[9] Although Miss Tandy is
more interested in Jack's satiric function than she is in his comic
totality, what separates Smith's work from that of his best imitator,

Charles Augustus Davis, is Smith's inclusion of details of folk culture and of traditional humor. By this means Smith achieves for Jack the inclusiveness of humor rather than the specialization of satire. Furthermore, Smith's approval in this rafting passage of Jackson's policies allows him a degree of warmth and kindness which rescues the details of common gesture and dialect from a merely belittling function.

South Carolina appointed February 1, 1833, as the day that it would put its Ordinance of Nullification into effect—the day the state would have the power to resist the federal government. On that evening, Jack wrote with comic simplicity that he was not dead; indeed, he had not been shot at once. The wild-animal imagery associated with James Blair is now modulated to tranquility; from South Carolina, Jack writes, "it was all still as a mouse" (200). This stillness followed three events: Congress passed the so-called Force Bill, authorizing the President to use the military to enforce revenue laws; Clay's compromise tariff passed; and, in response, South Carolina suspended the Ordinance of Nullification.

In Jack's final letter about the crisis, Smith presents some of his own political beliefs:

For some say there'll be no more fighting in the country while Mr. Clay lives, if it should be a thousand years. He's got a master knack of pacifying folks and hushing up quarrels as you ever see. He's stopt all that fuss in South Carolina, that you know was jest ready to blow the whole country sky high. He stept up to 'em in Congress and told 'em what sort of a Bill to pass, and they passed it without hardly any jaw about it. . . . And that isn't the only quarrel Mr. Clay has stopt. Two of the Senators, Mr. Webster and Mr. Poindexter, got as mad as March hairs at each other. . . . Well, after Mr. Clay got through with South Carolina, he took them in hand. He jest talked to 'em about five minutes, and they got up and went and shook hands with each other, and looked as loving as two brothers. (206 - 7)

This passage and others like it represent Smith's contribution to the popular image of Clay as the "Great Pacificator." Smith's belief in pacific solutions, in a devotion to calm, in gentlemanly conduct, and in faith in reason runs clearly through his work.

IV   *Shaking Hands for the President*

One of Smith's most memorable comic inventions was inspired by Jackson's tour in the spring, 1833, through Pennsylvania, New York, and New England. In Philadelphia, Jack writes, people arrived by the thousands to shake hands with the President:

. . . federalists and all, it made no difference. There was such a stream of 'em coming in that the hall was full in a few minutes, and it was so jammed up round the door that they couldn't get out again if they were to die. So they had to knock out some of the windows and go out t'other way.

The President shook hands with all his might an hour or two, till he got so tired he couldn't hardly stand it. I took hold and shook for him once in awhile to help him along, but at last he got so tired he had to lay down on a soft bench covered with cloth and shake as well as he could, and when he couldn't shake he'd nod to 'em as they come along. And at last he got so beat out, he couldn't only wrinkle his forehead and wink. Then I kind of stood behind him and reached my arm round under his and shook for him for about a half an hour as tight as I could spring. (213 - 14)

To have Jack shake hands for the President comically implies the insincerity of Jackson's relationship to the masses of the folk.

As Jack draws nearer to the Jacksonian presence, he becomes literally one of the President's hands to manipulate the voters. Psychically, the identification between the two figures becomes closer: both men are unfit to lead because they are selfish. To the conservative judgment of Seba Smith, the leader must submit selflessly to the functions of his role. George Washington's great personal sacrifices mirrored the new nation's highest hopes. If the leader cannot subdue in himself the impulse to egocentric self-aggrandizement, he becomes the tyrant-monster. In both Jack and Jackson, the fatal flaw is their inability to control natural selfishness.[10] The appearance of shaking hands is all there is to Jackson's supposed affection for common people.

Another meaning in this rich little scene is the President's almost total infirmity which is pictured as the slow, crumbling collapse of a man then sixty-six. Cheering crowds had lined his long triumphal procession, and reception committees and interminable banquets had filled his days and nights. He began to suffer a severe pain in the side and bleeding of his lungs, but he forced himself to remain erect and attentive. Smith's fiction, however, through an inventive comic stroke, focuses on the President's age and decay; the earnest concern of Jack's fantastic gesture devaluates and dismisses a feeble old man.

The fantasy of the episode was so comic and Jack's exaggerated admiration of the President was so lovingly supportive and so true

to the enthusiasms of masses of Jackson's real followers that the
sketch delighted Jackson's supporters as well as his opponents.
Ironically, Smith's design to dramatize the President's falseness and
infirmity pleased Jackson himself when it was read to him during
his most serious illness. As Marquis James reports,

> On his fourth day in Boston a severe cold and bleeding of the lungs con-
> fined the President to his bed in the Fremont House. Physicians bled him.
> Quincy entertained the patient by reading from Seba Smith of the Portland
> (Maine) *Courier*, whose letters over the name of Major Jack Downing were
> the most widely reprinted and plagiarized newspaper humor of the
> day. . . . In the present instance he assumed to be a member of the of-
> ficial touring party. His two most recent letters described incidents of the
> journey. At Philadelphia, when the President became exhausted by
> handshaking, the indispensable Major had stepped behind him and,
> thrusting his strong arm beneath Jackson's weary one, finished off the
> greetings as the President's understudy, with no one a whit the wiser.[11]

Again, richness of the scene enlarges its focus from the sharpness of
satire to the breadth of humor.

The harshest meanings of the episode inspired David Claypoole
Johnston, the illustrator of the 1833 edition of *The Life and
Writings of Major Jack Downing*. In his design for the scene,
Johnston draws the President in a near-recumbent position on a
divan; Jack, bending behind the piece of furniture, uses his left arm
to support Jackson; and his right hand is extended beneath
Jackson's limply dangling arm. Jackson's body is attenuated; his
eyes are almost closed; his face is deeply drawn. Altogether, his portrayal is very nearly corpselike.

As for the surrounding mass of people in the background,
Johnston, following the practice of William Hogarth and James
Gillray, presents disorderly, unregenerate mankind. Four figures
stand forth from the mass: to the left, an affected dandy primps in
the line; to the right, a grossly bewhiskered, ragged, beggarly figure
presents his back to the viewer. A cur, again a common image in
Hogarth's work for neglect and disorder, sniffs this character's un-
bathed foot through his broken boot; but this nearly faceless man,
more horrific than comic, follows only the principals in importance.
A successful office seeker, his clearly readable notice of appointment in his hip pocket, shakes Jack's hand extended for the President on the couch; and the man next in line is an unbuttoned, por-
cine creature with a heavy, animalistic face. More bluntly, and

without Smith's affection, Johnston's picture declares the disapproval of the moralist. In effect, the feeble, dying Jackson, calls forth to public life the low, teeming, disorderly humanity of America; and another like him is already half taking his place.

V *Unutterable Disappointment in Downingville*

Jackson's tour also called from Seba Smith one of his richest and most subtle presentations of the Downingville community. Smith's fiction is that the President, after appearing in Boston, Salem, and Concord, will visit Downingville to shake hands with Uncle Joshua, "that faithful old republican" (208 - 9). But after Jackson's collapse in Concord, the Major, alluding to the President's health and to party quarrels, writes that the visit is canceled. Downingville's unutterable disappointmment occasions Cousin Nabby's letter to the *Courier*, in which she creates the whole drama as the little community saw it. She does so without obvious political satire, but her portrayal is full of the humor of character, language, and folkways.

As Cousin Nabby writes it, notice of the President's visit came to Uncle Joshua. Sorting all other mail, opening his least important letters first, cutting himself a chew of tobacco, Uncle Joshua, by silence and delay, tantalizes the isolated community's hunger for news. Simultaneously, Smith has Cousin Nabby present the style of Uncle Joshua's own controlled, down East character: "We all stood tiptoe with our hearts in our mouths, and he must needs read it over to himself three times, chawing his old quid and once in awhile giving us a knowing wink, before he would tell us what was in it.— And he wouldn't tell us arter all, but, says he, you must all be ready to put the best side out Thursday morning; there'll be business to attend to, such as Downingville never see before" (223). Thus Uncle Joshua controls and communicates the occasion's emotion not by extravagance of language or movement but by silence, small gestures, and understatement—a style which intimates that the greatest excitement is unutterable.[12]

The festival of welcome is expressed by "washing and scrubbing and making new clothes and mending old ones and baking and cooking" (223). Since Jackson was to stay at Uncle Joshua's, Aunt Keziah prepared the reception:

She had every part of the house washed from garret to cellar, and the floors all sanded, and a bunch of green bushes put into all the fire places.

And she baked three ovens full of dried punkin pies, besides a few dried huckleberry pies, and cakes, and a great pot of pork and beans. But the worst trouble was to fix up the bed so as to look nice; for ant Keziah declared the President should have as good a night's lodging in her house as he had in New York or Boston. So she put on two feather beds on top the straw bed, and a bran new calico quilt that she made the first summer after she was married and never put it on a bed before. And to make it look as nice as the New York beds, she took her red silk gown and ripped it up and made a blanket to spread over the top. And then she hung up some sheets all round the bedroom, and the gals brought in a whole handful of roses and pinks and pinned 'em up round as thick as flies in August. (223 - 24)

The folkways of Downingville express the joy and honor of the occasion with an abundance of food, the promised comfort of many feather beds, the beauty of the red silk gown generously sacrificed for the occasion, and the fresh flowers brought by the girls. The room ready, the children washed and combed, and the villagers lining the road, the little world of common people awaits the great leader. But he never comes.

When Uncle Joshua arrives to tell them all to go home, the villagers express their anger—an attitude that contrasts with his earlier, intense, controlled delight:

My stars! what a time there was then. I never see so many folks boiling over mad before. Bill Johnson threw his gun over into the field as much as ten rods, and hopped up and down and struck his fists together like all possessed. Sargent Joel marched back and forth across the road two or three times, growing redder and redder, till he drew out his sword and fetched a blow across a hemlock stump and snapped it off like a pipe stem. Ant Keziash fell down in a conniption fit; and it was an hour before we could bring her tu and get her into the house.—And when she come to go round the house and see the victuals she had cooked up, and go into the bed-room and see her gown all cut up, she went into conniption fits again and had 'em half the night. (225)

The selection invites reading as an allegorical warning that the great leader will not come among the common people and as a fiction that celebrates the rich forms by which the folk life expresses itself. The sketch is detailed, circumstantial, and finely structured. Not only are the actions of cleaning, cooking, and decorating items of contemplation and esthetic pleasure in themselves, but they contrast the love and hospitality extended by the people to the disregard of their leader. Downingville's unutterable disappointment is most eloquently expressed.

Even the minor matter of traditional folk gestures is arranged in contrasting sets to show the community's change from pleasure in being recognized to destructive anger at being ignored. At the opening, Smith presents Uncle Joshua as methodically ordering the mail, as seating himself, as reading and rereading the announcement in silence, as chewing, and as winking to his attentive audience. At the end, he simply rides up and abruptly tells the villagers to go home. The concluding scene shifts focus to Bill Johnson's throwing his gun into the field and striking his fists together and to Sergeant Joel's breaking his sword—all traditional gestures of frustration and anger.

The appearance of the Jacksonian presence near Downingville implies, like the handshaking episode, not Jackson's closeness to the common people but his distance from them. Smith's earlier creation of Jack's national political aspirations implied that Jacksonian politics created in common folk ambitions that were certainly destructive and that were probably to be disappointed. In Downingville's disappointment, he repeats the theme of false hopes, of hopes that bring disorder and decay in society. The movement of this fable of a promise made and broken is from joy to anger, from concord to discord.

Behind these comic fictions lies Smith's recognition of the power of the Jacksonian presence. Davy Crockett applies the metaphors of royalty to the President. In the unfriendly political iconography of the time, Jackson often appears in robe and crown as King Andrew. The image implies not only his regal pride and imperial ambition but also the servile adulation of his followers. During these expansionist years, the masses of the American people opened great sources of energy for their tasks by envisioning themselves as God's chosen people.[13] National types and more often national leaders were apotheosized as instruments of Nature or of God in His creation of America's destiny. The deification of Jackson in legend, song, metaphor, and icon was as stirring to his followers as it was absurd or dismaying to his opponents.

Cartoonists daringly satirized this idolatry by caricaturing Jackson as the Saviour. A. J. Mason's title-page illustration for Charles Augustus Davis' imitations of Seba Smith in *Letters of J. Downing, Major,* presents Jackson as the central figure in a witty burlesque based on the Ascension. The lean, lantern-jawed, sour-faced President appears in the traditional place of Christ through an opening in clouds. Hat off, head inclined downward toward his people, he is surrounded by a glory of light. Below him and on either side of him are grotesque bumpkin angels who fling their hats into the air. The satire on idolatry is sharp and explicit. Smith's own technique is indirect and has less reliance on the fantastic and the grotesque, for his recurring treatment of the Jacksonian figure is to keep it homely and unbuttoned. But, when he touches the theme of Jackson as a Saviour figure, he manages, by his focus on Downingville's point of view, to create a solid sense of the weight and power of the unseen presence and to reject its virtue.

VI   Jack and the "Gineral" at Harvard

At its June, 1833, commencement, Harvard University conferred, as was the overseers' custom, an honorary Doctorate of Laws on the President. Jack's account of his participation became one of the most widely circulated and imitated of Smith's letters; and, according to John William Ward in *Andrew Jackson: Symbol for an Age*, it is the one that, perhaps, "most interests the modern students of Jack Downing."[14] The theme is Jackson's ignorance of academic traditions and of Latin. To the traditional ruling class, accustomed to the elegant literary accomplishments of the nation's first six presidents, this lack seemed one of the most painful of Jackson's shortcomings. When John Quincy Adams asked Harvard's President Quincy if the college could not avoid presenting the degree and was told it could not, the ex-President wrote in his diary that he "would not be present to witness the college's disgrace in conferring her highest literary honors upon a barbarian who could not write a sentence of grammar and hardly could spell his own name."[15]

Smith's fictional account, however, is neither bitter nor horrified but broadly comic:

Ye see when we were at Boston they sent word to us to come out to Cambridge, for they wanted to make the President a Doctor of Laws. What upon arth a Doctor of Laws was, or why they wanted to make the President one, I couldn't think. So when we come to go up to bed I asked the Gineral about it. And says I, Gineral, what is it they want to do to you out to Cambridge? Says he they want to make a Doctor of Laws of me. Well, says I, but what good will that do? Why, says he, you know Major Downing, there's a pesky many of them are laws passed by Congress, that are rickety things. Some of 'em have very poor constitutions, and some of 'em haven't no constitutions at all. So that it is necessary to have somebody there to Doctor 'em up a little, and not let 'em go out into the world where they would stan a chance to catch cold and be sick, without they had good constitutions to bear it. You know, says he, I have had to doctor the Laws considerable ever since I've been at Washington, although I wasn't a regular bred Doctor. (228)

The President's and Jack's literal interpretation of "Doctor" exposes their provincial ignorance of and indifference to academic honors. The punning on "constitution" and on "doctoring" expresses the conservative's judgment of Jackson's disregard for legality in his government.

Jackson's ignorance of Latin was Smith's second topic for comic fiction:

But, says he, Major, I feel a little kind of streaked about it after all; for they say they will go to talking to me in Latin, and although I studied it a little once, I dont know any more about it now than the man in the moon. And how I can get along in that case I dont know. I told him my way, when any body talked to me in a lingo that I didn't understand, was jest to say nothing, but look as knowing as any of 'em, and then they ginerally thought I knew a pesky sight more than any of 'em. At that the Gineral fetched me a slap on my shoulder, and haw hawed right out. Says he, Major Downing, you are the boy for me; I dont know how I should get along in this world if it wasn't for you. (228 - 29)

At the Latin speech, says Jack, the General was a little puzzled, but said nothing, only bowed slightly—but unfortunately, Jack guessed, at the wrong time, "for I could see some of the sassy students look up one side once in a while, and snicker out of one corner of their mouths. Howsomever, the Gineral stood it out like a hero. . . " (229). Historical accounts of the event differ: Jackson may have received his honor in silence; but Josiah Quincy wrote that there "were a few modest words, presumably in the vernacular, though scarcely audible, from the recipient of the doctorate."[16]

Jack's hypocritical solution, to fake knowledge in bows and to hide ignorance in silence, is open to multiple responses, for an author's intention may have little to do with what the reader sees in his work. Smith's amiable reduction of the President flattered the superiority of the educated, but it could equally excite the glee of the Jacksonian common man. The story was so good, Josiah Quincy wrote, in "showing how the man of the people could triumph over the crafts and subtleties of classical pundits, that all Philistia wanted to believe it."[17] The uneducated preferred to believe in the adequacy of common sense. For them, the story did not unmask Jackson's ignorance; instead, it showed the triumph of mother wit over the pretentions of useless formal education. To the folk judgment, Latin speeches to American audiences were an impertinence.

Disdain for Latin was, or quickly became, one of the themes of the new democratic style. In 1833 Davy Crockett wrote in his *Autobiography* that, when he first ran for office, he had to talk to people about "government, and an eternal sight of other things that I knowed nothing more about than I did about Latin, and law, and such things as that." Ten years later, Sam Slick expressed this feeling in blunt commercial imagery: "As for Latin and Greek, we don't valy it a cent." The folk feeling that Classical scholarship is not so valuable as curing wounds or growing potatoes arises in part from simple devotion to the immediately useful, but also in part from perception of its uses for snobbery and evasions. Some kinds of studies, as Unamuno puts it, mean cowardice, "cowardice in confronting the eternal problems . . . cowardice in stirring up the most profound restlessness of our eternal souls. This cowardice leads many to erudition, that opiate for disquieted spirits, that occupation rooted in spiritual sloth, an activity resembling the game of chess."[18] A similar perception led Henry Thoreau, himself a fine Classical scholar, to praise John Brown as an unlearned Humanist who "would have left a Greek accent slanting the wrong way, and righted up a falling Man."

Despite Smith's study of Greek and Latin and his pride in his college education, his creation of the episode gives more vigor and dignity to Jackson's misplaced bows than it does to the snickering of the students. With no implied claim that Latin is an enlarging or humanizing accomplishment, the speech becomes an empty form. The General is dignified for having "stood it out like a hero." Smith's own ambiguous attitude toward his creation clearly emerges from the episode. Later, when he turned his letters into a book, his burlesque dedication is to Jackson, and he had his publishers send copies of both the first and third editions to the President, copies that could in fact be called complimentary.[19]

VII   *A False Jack Downing*

This artistic willingness to give the President his due is one of the characteristics which separate Smith's letters from those of his most popular imitator, Charles Augustus Davis. Well-to-do iron merchant, friend of the Knickerbocker literati, and silk-stocking Whig, Davis appropriated Smith's creation to begin on June 25, 1833, a series of anti-Jackson letters in the *New York Daily Advertiser.*[20] As satire, Davis' letters are politically and economically sophisticated; as fictions, they are sharp caricatures; but they lack the richness and sympathy of Smith's work. Furthermore, Davis' New England dialect is so hastily formulated that his language is at times grotesque and at others tasteless; but his content is intellectually quick and witty.

Davis' letters (distinguished by the signature J. Downing, Major) were widely popular, and they frequently appeared in newspapers beside Smith's inventions dealing with the same events. Obviously editors and their readers were enjoying comparing the two. By October, 1833, Davis conceived the clever hoax of claiming that he had written the original Downing letters, apologized for their pretended inferiority by pleading inexperience, and announced he was issuing a volume of his early and late letters—a volume of both Smith's and his work. Alarmed, Seba Smith asked Davis' publisher not to include the authentic letters and declared that his own volume would appear within weeks.[21] Surely such immediate competition spurred Smith to a continued examination of his own artistry and meanings.

CHAPTER 5

The Life and Writings of Major Jack Downing

B Y creating the central character as fully as Smith had, he avoided the narrow specialization of the satiric persona. Instead, he had developed a point of view from a second culture which, limited though it was, had its own tone and its own moral and esthetic values. Smith's conservatism and his love of scholarship were balanced by strong affection for and appreciation of the values of the folk culture from which he himself had developed. Simultaneously, he had a strong intuitive perception of the nature and function of folk humor: its characteristic devotion to freedom and play; its celebration of vitality; its impulse to doubt the perfection and permanence of official culture; its love of variety, excitement, even chaos and destruction; and its festive character. This combination of down East folk culture with the culture of folk humor creates the distinctive tonal quality of the Downing letters.

Finally, and most broadly, Jack's character represents Seba Smith's struggle with Michel de Crèvecoeur's question: What is, then, the American? Jack's freedom, activism, and unquestioning faith in himself, while blind, are, as Emerson would shortly say, spiritually marvelous conditions. To some extent, Jack Downing represents Seba Smith's attraction to a new moral being; for he dramatizes what Lewis P. Simpson calls "the primary shaping force in the American existence: the complex psychic struggle of faith and doubt concerning the American condition as regenerate."[1] Subordinate and wavering as it is, Jack's dimension as comic New World man grows perceptibly as Smith creates his adventures.

I *Jack Conceives Presidential Ambitions*

By the summer of 1833, Jack Downing was nationally popular through newspaper reprints, and Smith had decided to turn the letters into a book. His first problem was what form to give his existing materials. Ingeniously, he enlarged his basic burlesque: he would let Jack aspire to the Presidency, and the letters could most naturally, with the addition of a long mock-autobiographical introduction, be re-created as a burlesque campaign *Life and Writings*. After a friend had approached a Boston publisher for Smith, publishers Lilly, Wait, Colman, & Holden wrote to Smith on September 11, 1833, to say that they had learned that he thought "of having the Letters and a Memoir of 'Major Downing' published in the Book form" and that, as they were "in want" of an amusing book, they would be pleased to publish the work with eight or ten engravings. Smith answered at once, and within a week the firm offered good terms for a first edition of two thousand copies.[2]

Smith had Jack in his letter of July 20, 1833, begin his discussion of his presidential ambitions. This letter recounts a quarrel between Jack and Martin Van Buren that is designed to show Van Buren's jealousy of the President's friendship with Jack. "Mr. Van Buren said the President had dishonored the country by placing a military Major on half pay before the second officer of the government. . . . He said he thought it was a fine time of day if a raw jockey from an obscure village away down east . . . was going to throw the Vice President of the United States and the heads of Departments into the back ground." (235). The quarrel culminates in Van Buren's charge that Jackson is plotting to support Jack for the presidential nomination.

Dizzied by this high prospect, Jack recalls prophecies of greatness. His father had once doubtfully observed to an old woman telling fortunes, "here's Jack, you haven't told his fortune yet, and I dont spose it's worth a telling, for he's a real mutton-headed boy" (237). But the fortuneteller had said, with what Jack took for sibylline indirection, that he would be a famous "climber" some day and get "to the top of the ladder" (237). In a subsequent letter, Jack writes that the President has indeed slowly revealed some deep plan for him:

At last, said he, Major Downing, were you ever told that you resembled Daniel Webster?
    Why, Gineral, says I, how do you mean, in looks or what?
    Why perhaps a little of both says he, but mostly in looks. (245)

The President discloses his fear that the nullification controversy will lead to a civil war. He believes the Union can be preserved only by two conditions: if Webster becomes President and if Jack leads in war. Jack, who is disappointed, is shocked that Webster, an old Hartford Convention Federalist, should even be considered.

But, when Jackson reminds Jack that Webster had joined him in the South Carolina crisis and could keep the country out of the jaws of nullification, Jack accepts the sacrifice of his immediate ambition if the editor of the *Portland Courier* and his Uncle Joshua also concur with Jackson's views: "If they think, it's best to have Daniel for President we'll have him in, and I'll take my turn afterwards; for seeing the people are bent on having me for President I wont decline, though if it is thought best that I should wait a little while, I wont be particular about that. I'm willing to do that which will be best for the country" (250). Again Jack innocently unites his own ambition and the good of his country. His banal cant, Smith thought, presented Jacksonian democracy's essential flaw.

II   *Sam Patch*

From about one hundred items, Smith selected seventy for the book. Unfortunately, he did not revise his letters to shorten the paragraphs, he did not paragraph in conversation, and he did not use quotation marks. Therefore, separating the dialogue from Jack's text is difficult, particularly for the modern reader who is accustomed to a helpful use of space on the page. Also contributing to the general structural looseness of the book was Smith's decision to include some of his poetry, and to attribute it to Jack. Most popular of the two poems included was the concluding doggerel biography of Sam Patch, an American folk hero whom Jack recognized as a kindred spirit. A poor New England boy who, like Jack, aspired vaguely to greatness, Patch decided

> And if he would become renown'd,
>   And live in song or story,
> Twas time he should be looking round
>   For deeds of fame and glory. (263)

Having as his motto, "Some things can be done as well as others," Sam undertook to prove whatever it was that his saying meant by daring feats of leaping into water from great heights. His career ended in a fatal attempt to jump the Genessee Falls in 1829.

The poem, which had been published earlier in the *Courier*, was such a great success that it passed into the folk tradition and appeared later as a broadside. Richard M. Dorson, in a fine study of

the whole Sam Patch legend, speculates as to why this figure so cap-
tivated the American people in the 1830's and 1840's: "For that
public Sam was a 'natural,' an original in the flesh. . . . With the
squat name, the senseless bravado, the nonsense sayings, the
common-man origin, the fondness for brag, antics, drink, and
danger, and the death-in-action, the historic Patch possessed attributes for American apotheosis equalled by few folk-hero
prototypes. Like Crockett, Fink, and Mose, his contemporaries,
Sam reflected the ebullient Jacksonian United States."[3] Jack's
choice of Sam Patch as a model of the heroic life effectively adds to
Smith's portrait of him.

Patch's career also bemused a modern American poet, William
Carlos Williams; for Sam appears in *Paterson*. A recent Williams
critic sees Patch as "indifferent and self-destructive" because he is
"motivated only by a desperate emotional impetus that is too innocent—or ignorant—to accept limitation."[4] Jack and Sam, two
American folk heroes, both illuminate Smith's vision of Jacksonian
America as unleashing vital but undirected and essentially destructive ambition.

With Jack's need for a campaign *Life and Writings* established,
Seba Smith went to Boston to see his book through the press. The
work was hurried not only because the letters were at a flood tide of
popularity but also because competition was growing. According to
the publishers, a pirated edition of Smith's letters was in the press in
Philadelphia, and another volume of letters by Charles Augustus
Davis, Smith's most talented imitator, would shortly appear in New
York.

III *A Campaign Autobiography*

In Boston, Smith wrote his important opening section—the introductory autobiography which is again Jack's presentation of
himself to the world in his own semiliterate language. Like the
letters, the mock autobiography presents concretely the self-
centered quality of Jack's character. Jack displays, as he sees them,
the remarkable qualities of his experiences; and his story contains
humorous elements of unintentional self-betrayal. Jack's character
in this introduction is generally congruent with what Smith had
created throughout the letters, but the historical and cultural
background is significantly enriched. For readers of the book, Smith
provides cultural authorization for many of Jack's characteristics.

His self-satisfied provinciality arises from the traditional folk feeling that he was born in the center of creation, the navel of the world. With the tedious specificity of the folk narrator (here, as in the letters, a sense of the spoken voice is pervasive), Jack locates Downingville for the world: "It is about three miles from the main road as you go back into the country, and is *jest about in the middle of down east*" (19). From the center of the world, the folk hero ventures forth.

Jack's goodness is qualified by his egotism and by his ignorance. Smith returns to this theme in Jack's account of the life of his grandfather. The whole passage is rich in its sense of tradition, generous sympathy, and the significance of effort in ambition: "As I said afore, my grandfather, old Mr. Zebedee Downing, was the first settler in Downingville. Bless his old heart, he's living yet, and although he is eighty six years old, he attended a public caucus for the good of his country about two years ago, and made a speech . . . " (21). All his life Jack's grandfather enjoyed recounting his part in the "fatigue of Burgwine" under General Horatio Gates, but Smith's restrained tone toward martial achievements appears in the old man's impressions as the troops moved forward in their victory over the British: "And then, O marcy, such a sight I never see before and never want to again: stepping over the dead bodies, and the poor wounded wretches wallowing in their blood, mangled all to pieces, and such screeches and groans, some crying out dont kill me, dont kill me, and others begging us to kill 'em to put 'em out of misery. O, it was enough to melt the very heart of stone, said my grandfather . . . " (24).

The vision of war is not triumphant and egocentric but deeply sympathetic and humane. His father, too, Jack recalls, was a mild-mannered man who scarcely spoke a harsh word. Jack's attention to his father's mildness and to his grandfather's sympathy and pity for his enemies implies that his own martial spirit is not rooted in cultural violence or hatred but in inexperience and in love of adventure and reputation. The mild and the humane in Jack's background make mournful the decay in his own character. The passage not only is Smith's tribute to sympathy but also serves to contrast the Jacksonian violence to follow.

Jack's wavering capacity for pity is further presented in his filial devotion to his father. Like his Uncle Joshua, Jack did not care for work: "When I got to be considerable of a boy I used to have to work with father on the farm. But it always seemed to go rather against my grain . . . " (31). Rural folk humor abounds in jokes which offer laziness as the root of ambition to rise in the world, but Jack's shifts to avoid work are never callous if he can see the consequences of his laziness: "for after I got old enought to think more about it, it used to hurt my feelings to see the old gentleman work so hard. And many a time when he has taken hold of a hard job to do, I have gone to him and took it out of his hands, and said, now father you go into the house and set down and rest you . . . " (32). Jack's sympathy is as real as his laziness, but his perception is a burden. Only adventure and ignorance enable him to preserve his innocent ease.

Jack's recollections of his grandfather also honor his derivation from the pioneering tradition in the down East experience: "When he got through sogering in the revolutionary war, he took a notion he'd go and pick him out a good lot of land away down east to settle, where there was land enough to be had jest for the whistling for it, and where his boys would have a chance to do something in the world" (26 - 27). Deep in the Maine woods beyond the last road's end, Jack's grandfather found his land. Against the trunk of a "great oak tree" he turned his wagon over, piled brush around it for temporary shelter, and set to clearing:

But that old oak never was cut down; it's the very same one that stands out a little ways in front of grandfather's house now. And poor old grandmother as long as she lived, for she's been dead about five years, always made a practice once a year, when the day come round that they first camped under the old oak, to have the table carried out and set under the tree, and all hands, children and grand-children, had to go and supper there, and the good old lady always used to tell over the whole story how she slept eight nights under the waggon, and how they were the sweetest nights' rest she ever had. (27)

The annual supper becomes a ritual that commemorates the family's appropriation of a new home. The great oak is preserved as a symbol of the sheltering land; the ceremony celebrates the joy of the pioneering venture; Jack's record expresses his satisfaction in his place and his sense of tradition, which he loves even as he escapes it in his picaresque wanderings.

After grandfather Zebedee builds his cabin, he sets out his crops and garden: "Corn, and potatoes, and punkins, and beans, and squashes, and round near the house he planted water-millions, and mush-millions, and cowcumbers, and beats and carrots and tarnips;

and grandmother carried out a whole apron full of seeds of all kinds of arbs that ever grew in old Massachusetts, and sowed 'em all round, and they come up as thick as hops" (28). The cultivation of food in variety and of herbs for flavor presents the festive richness of Jack's folk culture, just as the commemorative supper presents its ceremonial and emotional richness.

In spite of Jack's feeling about the worth of his family, his discontent, well-grounded in the comic contradictions of his character, never leaves him—and least of all while working: "But let me be doing what I would, whether it was hoeing potatoes, or pitching hay, or making stone wall, or junking and piling logs, I never could feel exactly easy; something seemed to keep ringing in my ears all the time, and saying I was made to do something else in the world besides this" (33 - 34).

When the lazy Jack's yearnings are in time answered, his final call to adventure is again expressed by Smith in terms of folk culture. First the old fortuneteller's comically ambiguous prophecy is anticipated—that Jack is a "climber" and will get to the top—and then his father has a strange, prophetic dream. In his dream, his son appears with a plant that is growing out of his head and that is bearing leaves, buds, and beautiful flowers.[5] The vision deeply affects his father, causes his mother to cry, and makes Jack feel that the day will come when Downingville will not be big enough to hold him. The fairy-tale imagery of the dream possesses a fine metaphoric logic: it implies that Jack will realize himself in the same way a bush realizes itself—naturally, effortlessly, and beautifully. The comic prophecy that his life would flower in an unusual destiny grows out of Jack's own lazy actions and yearnings, is shared by his parents, and is authorized by the folk culture's respect for fortunetellers and dreams.

After Jack travels to the city, he gets advice from Mr. Smith, the editor of the *Portland Courier* and the *Family Reader*. Thus soberly, and to no very great effect, except for the playful, Seba Smith appears from time to time among his fictional and historical characters. Smith encourages Jack to seek his fortune, but he warns him about the sharp traders in Huckster's Row. Jack, however, decides to test himself. In burlesque of the legendary hero's trial, he tricks a storekeeper out of two cents. The trick is traditional: he asks the storekeeper for two cents' worth of biscuits; trades the biscuits for cider; and, when asked to pay for the cider, claims he gave the biscuits for them.[6] Next day Jack pays the two cents. Smith enjoyed the traditional trick, but he did not wish to present Jack as a simple cheater. The dream and the trick, as well as other passages in the introductory portion, testify to Seba Smith's enlarging interest in the details and the meanings of folk culture.

IV *"a queer phiz"*

The illustrations for his first book engaged Smith's earnest concern, and the letters he exchanged with his wife about them provide external evidence of his conception of Jack's meaning. When his publisher commissioned David Claypoole Johnston (1798 - 1865), then living in Boston, to design and execute the illustrations, they made an excellent choice; for Johnston was, according to art historian David Tatham, "the first American comic artist to have a sustained and popular career."[7] Although influenced by the ideas and the techniques of James Gillray and George Cruikshank, Johnston increasingly turned from 1824 on to American topics and types. Militia officers, drunks, food-faddists, Abolitionists, and a great number of other contemporary creatures and events were caricatured by Johnston's pen. Because Johnston was richly literary in his interests, he so impressed Seba Smith that he asked the artist to read Jack's mock autobiography. Smith later wrote uneasily to Elizabeth that he feared Johnston was not pleased. Johnston was, in fact, a harder satirist than Smith.

Spurred by the competition of the volumes announced in both Philadelphia and New York, Smith's publisher urged him to furnish subjects quickly for the illustrations.[8] In mid-October, Smith wrote Elizabeth:

Johnston has made a drawing for the Major's portrait and put it into the hands of the engraver. It is a queer phiz. I cannot tell by seeing it on the block how I shall like it. It represents the Major sitting at a table writing letters, with one finger up by the side of his nose to help him think. He has two or three letters written, one addressed to Uncle Josh, another to Cousin Nabby, etc. His military dress and sword hang up by him. He is rather a slick headed knowing looking chap, but I cannot tell whether I shall feel satisfied with it until I see an impression of the engraving.[9]

After Seba Smith saw the impression, he wrote Elizabeth that he thought she would not like it: "His face has a little too much of the caricature about it."[10] Despite Smith's use of caricature and burlesque, he felt that good taste demanded more reserve and understatement than the exuberant Johnston had allowed himself. Smith's esthetic doctrine implies the influence of the eighteenth-century concept of the amiable humorist.

His guess about Elizabeth's response to Johnston's picture, which he quickly sent her, proved to be correct. She wrote: "The portrait of the Major I don't like. I have not shown it to anyone. . . . The look is not honest. Jack is shrewd, but is he not honest? The eye is a little too much turned, the person too lean, and the countenance too sheepish; tell Johnson [sic] there is no necessity to make him so mortal homely. . . . Don't let this one go in without revision, for I am afraid it will give others the same sensation of disappointment."[11] To support her feeling, Elizabeth added that she had shown the picture to Smith's mother who had observed that she had thought the Major was a better looking man. Some sense of family identification emerges from the letters.

Seba Smith's disapproval of Johnston's caricature and Elizabeth's timid hope that Jack could be considered honest and should not be pictured as thin and ugly declare a shared judgment about him. Jack's association with the President of the United States was intended to be reductive; Jack's ambitions were intended to be absurd and even dangerous; but Jack was not intended to be a grotesque or unregenerate rustic. He represents another culture—one unsuited for leadership but one with its own values. There is something in Jack, Smith cannot say what, something indefinite, but large perhaps, that caricature does violence to.

V *Iconography*

Not only did Smith's letters call forth a host of literary imitators, but Jack Downing swiftly passed into the common American iconography. D. C. Johnston himself redrew Jack for his *Scraps No. 5* (1834) with a less wrinkled, grinning countenance. An extensive series of lithography cartoons signed "Zek Downing, Neffu to Major Jack Downing" but done in many manners, apparently by several hands, shows in some "a very original talent."[12] By 1838 a perceptive and witty correspondent for the London *Bentley's Miscellany* reported that Jack Downings were as ubiquitous in the United States as heads of John the Baptist in Italian monasteries.[13] "The Major Downing of the cartoons," writes William Murrell in his *History of American Graphic Humor*, "came very close to a personification of the American people; and he figured in drawings . . . for fully thirty years."[14]

Some of the graphic conceptions were strongly imaginative. One reproduced by Murrell shows Jackson and the Major standing together while about and above them float "rings of glory," an obvious thrust at idolatory of Jackson. The Boston *Globe* in 1845 describes one of the most unusual Jack Downings: an ambitious oil portrait at the Athenaeum Gallery. The face, the critic wrote, "beams with a characteristic expression of sly humor of a shrewd, thriving, full blooded yankee. It is a sort of humanized Silenus, with a breadth and vividness of sensual roguery in the expression of the mouth, which Rubens would have turned to good account in one of his Bachanalian groups."[15] Seba Smith's creation set up a powerful attraction that evoked a varied host of graphic and literary imitators and interpreters. Jack's liberating egotism, his vigorous pursuit of the easy job, his indomitable innocence and ease appealed widely as qualities somewhere near the center of the new American character.

VI   *Jack's Fate*

By early December, 1833, at the latest, *The Life and Writings of Major Jack Downing, of Downingville, Away Down East in the State of Maine, Written by Himself*, was for sale in the bookshops. Neither Smith's nor Johnston's name was given on the title page, but both appeared comically in the text. The volume contained the burlesque "My Life," seventy letters, two poems, an appendix including six spurious letters, and, probably, six illustrations by Johnston. Within weeks a third edition was reset with at least four new illustrations, an additional letter commenting on the first edition, and a very few minor corrections.

In July, 1834, the Smiths established the *Downing Gazette* which carried letters by Jack and to him from his family and others, including Davy Crockett. The material is sharply critical of Jackson.[16] When the *Gazette* ended as Jackson's term drew toward its close, the May 26, 1836, issue published details about Major Downing's illness of consumption and about his death in Downingville at the age of forty-two. Smith did not again use the figure, so closely identified with Andrew Jackson, until 1840 when, in New York, he created an account of Jack's "marvelous resurrection" for *The New World*.[17]

CHAPTER 6

New York: The Literary Marketplace

In private life, Seba Smith achieved the greatest rise in his
fortunes and experienced the most disappointing fall during the
1830's. The decade opened with his successful establishment of two
Portland newspapers, and his creation of Jack Downing made him
nationally popular. Although offended that other writers should appropriate his creation for their fictions and politics, Smith never
struggled to attach his own name to the Jack Downing figure. The
Jack Downing who became a national household word, whose
character achieved mythic proportions in American culture, was
never exploited by Smith to establish his own name in the way, say,
that Davy Crockett and his supporters worked to establish his fortunes on the fictional Davy's power.[1]

I *Financially Adrift*

Popular as the Downing books were, the financial failure of
publisher Lilly, Wait, Colman, & Holden robbed Seba Smith of the
income he had hoped to receive from his work. With five little boys
to rear, he decided to invest what money he had and could borrow
in land speculation. He became a large owner of undeveloped
Maine woodland. When financial loss threatened, Elizabeth urged
that they "leave all, take our library, chattels, and children, go into
the wilderness, build up a log cabin, and there live, educate, and
bring up our boys to manly toil and simple habits."[2] Smith, with
some experience of frontier life, rejected this Arcadian proposal.

To pay their debts, Smith sold his interest in the *Portland
Courier,* and the family went to live with his parents in the seaport
town of Boothbay, where, in spite of his sadness over the accidental
death of Rolvin, the Smiths' second son, Seba kept doggedly at his
writing. He completed a novel, *Esther Wylie,* which he later dis-
carded; he finished half of *Powhatan,* a long romantic historical

poem; and he wrote two stories later published in the volume '*Way Down East*.

Then another chance to make a quick fortune interrupted Smith's literary activities: his sister's husband, a Mr. Beath, invented a machine to clean the fibers of Sea Island cotton. In a gesture as uninformed and as hopeful as Jack Downing's journey to Washington, Smith invested his last thousand dollars in taking the brother-in-law, the cotton gin, and his own wife and children to South Carolina to interest cotton planters in the invention. The family spent the early part of 1839 in Charleston, but at the first exhibition of the machine it was declared impracticable.

In lowest fortunes now, the family returned not to Portland but to New York. The Smiths had decided to live by their writing but to take in boarders also when doing so was necessary to meet household expenses. With the spread of elementary education and cheap printing, literature had become a commodity; and New York City was the center of a flourishing magazine market. The Smiths at once set about learning what material was wanted by the numerous periodicals and how they could please the editors. Quickly Seba managed to place some of his letters in the *New York Mirror*, one of the leading city weeklies, which was devoted, it proclaimed, to literature and to the fine arts.

II   John Smith's Letters

John Smith's Letters with "Picters" to Match, Seba Smith's second book, developed from another series of mockrural letters. Early in 1839 the *Mirror* had printed an awkward comic essay ridiculing the name John Smith and advising its owner to change it. Smith's quick reply, printed in the same weekly, reveals his acute sensitivity to his commonplace name. Changing the family name, his letter hints, had already been discussed. In fact, as has been stated before, Elizabeth was soon signing her name Oakes Smith; and she later formalized her rejection of Smith's name by having the children's name legally changed to Oaksmith. Smith's reply to the *Mirror*'s comic advice unites the prospect of his own loss of name with Charles Augustus Davis' theft of not only the character but of the name of Jack Downing. Although Smith was angered by Davis' theft and was pained by Elizabeth's contempt for his own name, his John Smith letters sustain his amiable tone. Nostalgia and satire on female vanity serve to express his private feelings.

Smith's family perturbations are an example of early nineteenth-century American identity anxiety. At least one foreign observer of American ways, Francis Lieber, "ridiculed the constant name changes that were designed to suggest a respectable origin."[3] In their larger meaning, the John Smith letters are social satire about one of the manias of the era which Lieber called "a diseased anxiety" about the forms of distinction that existed simultaneously with an indifference to its substance and with a denial of any concern about it. James Fenimore Cooper in *Home as Found* (1838), that "catalogue of the infinite varieties of provincial deformity" as James Grossman calls it, also ridicules the American passion for name changing. He has a woman ask her neighbor to borrow her better sounding name for use on a trip to Utica. The damage to the name, the borrower assures the lender, will be paid in money.[4]

The John Smith of Seba Smith's first letter is a middle-aged village squire, a selectman, a surveyor of the roads, a twice-elected representative to the state legislature, and a member of the school committee. He is proud of being descended from Captain John Smith in a straight line of John Smiths, except for his father, who was James Smith:

I'll tell you how it happened. When my grandfather, whose name was John, carried my father to meetin' to be christened, it happened that the same day his cousin John Smith carried two of *his* children to be christened. And when the minister was ready, my grandfather, bein' a very perlite man, beckoned to his cousin John to carry his children up first. So he carried 'em up, and good old parson John Smith, who preached in grandfather's parish then, whispered to him as he handed up the first child, and asked him its name. His name is John, said my grandfather's cousin. So the parson christened him John. The second child was then handed up, and the parson whispered again and asked its name. His name is John, said my grandfather's cousin. The good old parson shook his head, and whispered again, and told him he had christened the other one John. My grandfather's cousin shook his head too, and told the parson to never mind, but christen him John; "for," says he, "if I had a hundred children, I would call them all John." So finding there was no turning him, the parson christened the second child John. Then my grandfather went up with his child; and I've heard my grandmother say that his face was red as a blaze all the way goin' up to the pulpit. Well, the minister whispered to him and asked him what the child's name was. Grandfather choked a little, and, says he, "I was going to call him John, but I think we have had Johns enough for one day; you may christen him James." (28 - 29)

The mechanical fixation that leads to abandonment of the rational function of naming belongs to the English tradition of amiable eccentricities. In fact, the mild persistence of John Smith's grandfather's cousin and the preoccupation with names recall Uncle Toby and Tristram's father in Laurence Sterne's *Life and Opinions of Tristram Shandy.* The dramatic presentation of the homely ceremony—with its gestures, beckonings, handing up of infants, inclining of heads, whispering—is simple and graphic. The rapid, idiomatic movement of the sentences and the repetition of word and phrase are also part of the eccentric humor of the passage.

By the fourth letter, Smith turns to national affairs. Using the technique of the Downing letters, he presents the Aroostook War through the eyes of rustic observers. The boundary between Maine and New Brunswick had been in question since the 1783 peace treaty; but, after Maine became a state in 1820, it made land grants to settlers along the Aroostook River. In the winter of 1838 - 39, when Canadian lumberjacks entered the disputed territory and began cutting timber, Maine Governor John Fairfield sent Rufus McIntire as land agent to expel the Canadians. Instead, the Canadians arrested McIntire; and both Maine and New Brunswick then summoned their militias. In John Smith's fourth letter of March 8, 1839, he turns from the village and from family history to describe the drafting of the militia at Smithville.

The excitement of the draft, the village's rustic method of drawing black and white beans from a bowl to select militiamen, the varied responses to excitement and danger, and the mixed pride and sorrow when the sixteen-year-old son enlists—all are conveyed in an understated colloquial style so skillful that the sketch is one of Smith's most memorable productions. The episode opens with the assembled three generations of the family reading the newspaper accounts of the boundary dispute. Grandfather compares the people's responses with those of Revolutionary days, and young John is stirred to intense excitement. On grandfather's assurance that war will come and the the militia will be drafted, they go uneasily to bed but not to rest.

In the dead of the night, a heavy knock awakens the sleeping family. It is the sergeant announcing that the governor's orders have come and that the draft will be held at Wilson's Tavern at 2.00 o'clock. A.M. so that the company may leave for Bangor at 8.00 o'clock. At the tavern, the local militia is represented by a bowl of eighty beans—twenty black—to answer the call for twenty men. Most respond with courage; one collapses in fear and is excused; the village braggart tries both to stay home and to keep his reputation. To fill the latter's place, young John enlists with his father's reluctant consent. Next day, when John marches away, his proud but distraught family stands along the roadside.

This homely story of war's intimate meaning is sustained by a careful pattern of sound imagery. The men's reading voices at the opening are counterpointed by the women's sighs. The heavy knock at the door comes at midnight. Before John and his father are dressed, they hear the drum beating from the tavern. At their return, the men's excited voices are answered by a rising series of cries from the women. John's mother weeps quietly. "The older gals, they cried considerable louder; and some of the younger children, that didn't hardly understand what the trouble was about, sot in and screamed as loud as they could bawl" (66). The effect of the sound imagery is to emphasize the varied human responses—the feelings of love, concern, and misery.

Letters V, VI, and VII contain young John's accounts of the militia's adventures in the Maine woods. John recounts the excitement of the march, the reception by villagers along the way, the meeting with Governor Fairfield, the joining with Colonel Jarvis at Fitzherbert's farm, the capture of some Canadian loggers, the comic pursuit and capture of a moose, and finally the narrator's safe return to his family. The anticipation of battle, the real bravery of the soldiers in its awkward reality, and the safe return give the series a slight plot.

The political aspect of the letters ends with John's report that Winfield Scott averted war by calming Governor John Fairfield of Maine and Sir John Harvey of New Brunswick. "At any rate," young John says, "I guess, between Gineral Scott and our company, that war is put a stop to. . . .They say that Gineral Scott is a master feller to talk to folks and keep 'em from fighting; but if they *will* fight, they must look out, for he'll put it into 'em jist like old Gineral Jackson" (133). The praise of a strong authority figure as peacemaker closes the structure of political meanings in the book.

Another element that gives unity to *John Smith's Letters* is a recurrent festive motif. In Letter I, the family is drawn around the fireplace in winter, drinking cider and eating Smith's "fine winter apples" (19). Apples appear as a constant source of delight in Seba Smith's writing, particularly in winter scenes. In Letter IV, after the draft, the women and children, with touchingly burdensome affection, stuff young John's knapsack with doughnuts, apples, and pieces of cake "after their mother had crammed in as much as she thought he could carry. . ." (73). This ceremonial preparation for the journey is an outward and visible sign of the inward love that the family feels for John. In the following letter, the soldiers are invited into a farm house to drink the farmer's cider while they eat their food. At the end of Letter V, the governor invites the militia to bivouac in one of the lobbies of the state house in Augusta, where he sends them food. "And we fared well, too, I can tell you—a plenty of bread and meat, and hot coffee, and a basket of apples" (85). Apart from the militia's feasting, a detailed description of the Canadian loggers' dinner is presented: "There was six of 'em, and they was all setting round the table eating their dinners. They had a great large milk-pan in the middle of the table full of baked beans and three or four pounds of fat pork on the top of it; and a kettle of soup on one end of the table, and bread and potatoes and so on, all over the table" (105).

The most festive scene of all is, appropriately, described in the last letter. The village plans to celebrate the safe and triumphant return of its soldiers with a public dinner. At twelve o'clock, the villagers blow the horn at the tavern, where fifty are gathered: "A better dinner a body couldn't hardly wish to see, even on thanksgiving day. There was biled salt beef, and pork and potatoes and cabbage, and pots of baked pork and beans, and baked Indian puddings, and fried pork and eggs, and pickled cowcumbers, and punkin pies, and fried sassages, and soused tripe, and roast spareribs, and stewed apple, and butter, and cheese, and hot bread, and cider, and I don't know what all" (135). The setting in the public tavern, the crowd of people, the cheerful community spirit, the grotesquely triumphant toasts, the repeated laughter and cheering, and the detailed enumeration of the foods unite to create a gaily festive ending. Universally, the banquet with its free, jocular speech, celebrates not only community, but also our common biological aspiration to life and abundance.[5]

John Smith's Letters with "Picters" to Match, a small volume of 139 pages which grew out of the newspaper series, was published late in 1839 by Samuel Colman of New York. The book appeared with a comic illustration on its cardboard cover depicting Captain John Smith's shield which is flanked by John Smith Tenth and Cousin Debby and is surmounted by the Smith family tree. Within

the volume are included a frontispiece and an illustration for each
letter except the fifth one. All were designed under the pseudonym
"Fungus," but they were engraved by three separate hands.
Carefully executed and printed on fine paper, the illustrations are
part of the charm of the book—comic, vigorous, and amiably
grotesque.

III   Minor Members of the Literati

By the 1840's, New York led both Boston and Philadelphia as the
nation's center for the publication of periodicals; and writers
swarmed in the city "like mites in a cheese, numerous and active."[6]
Elizabeth and Seba found a ready market for their talents, and both
through their works and the force of Elizabeth's personality the
Smiths came to be recognized as minor members of the New York
literati. In 1842 they moved to South Brooklyn. At Cheever Place,
Mrs. Oakes Smith, as she was now calling herself, held her literary
salon on Sunday evenings. These occasions commanded the
presence of such then famous persons as Sarah J. Hale, Frances
Osgood, Sarah Helen Whitman, Horace Greeley, Elizabeth's
devoted admirer Charles Fenno Hoffman, Henry T. Tuckerman,
William Cullen Bryant, and Edgar Allan Poe. Poe attended
Elizabeth's gatherings frequently, was impressed by her beauty and
manner, and reviewed her poem *The Sinless Child* (1842) very
favorably. Finding Seba perhaps less charming, Poe was less
generous to him.[7]

During the decades of the 1840's and 1850's, Smith contributed
to journals and giftbooks and undertook a great amount of editorial
work. Besides the *New York Mirror,* he wrote for *The Knickerbocker,* edited by the faithful Whig Lewis Gaylord Clark;
Snowden's *Ladies' Companion; Godey's Lady's Book; Graham's
Magazine;* the *Southern Literary Messenger;* Greeley's *New
Yorker;* Park Benjamin's *New World;* and the *Literary Emporium*—all the best-known journals of the time.[8]

Between 1825 and 1865, more than a thousand giftbooks and
literary annuals appeared in the United States. Printed on fine
paper, with elegant illustrations and with specially designed bind-
ings, these volumes were "ideally suited to an aspiring middle
class. They appealed to the eye and the heart rather than to the
mind; they were handsome and costly; they were 'artistic' and
'refined.' They met a demand for 'culture.' "[9]

The prose and the poetry printed in the giftbooks did not compete with that in serious magazines. Sentimental, genteel, such work was tailored for the female mind, as the mid-nineteenth century conceived that mind. Both Elizabeth and Seba could produce material exactly right for such miscellanies, and their work is well represented in a number of collections of what Mrs. Lydia Sigourney called "luxurious literature."[10] Smith wrote for *The Portland Sketch Book* (1836), *The Gift* (1843 and 1844), *The Christian Souvenir* (1843 and 1844), *The Wintergreen* (1844), *The Fountain* (1847), and *The May Flower* (1847). In addition, he edited *Dewdrops of the Nineteenth Century Gathered and Preserved in Their Brightness and Purity* (1846), which was apparently popular since it was reissued in 1847 and in 1854 under the original title and in 1848 under two new names: *The Gift of Friendship* and *The Keepsake*.[11] *Dewdrops*, like most volumes of its kind, contained reprinted items: Smith included material by Longfellow, William Cullen Bryant, John Greenleaf Whittier, Leigh Hunt, and Thomas Hood. He and Elizabeth made up the rest of the miscellany by supplying ten items of their own.[12]

During the 1840's and 1850's Smith also held editorial positions on about ten New York magazines, several of them too insignificant and too short-lived to be even mentioned in Frank Luther Mott's monumental *History of American Magazines*.[13] The journals Smith was associated with were eclectic, making up a good portion of their contents from clippings from other magazines and books, with little or no attention to copyrights. What original items they did include were frequently supplied by the editorial staff, and on occasion Smith, Mrs. Oakes Smith, and their sons Appleton, Edward, Sidney, and Alvin all contributed their talents.[14]

The first of Smith's own ventures into magazine publication to have any success was *Rover: A Weekly Magazine of Tales, Poetry, and Engravings*, which appeared from 1843 to 1845. A budding writer who called on Smith at the *Rover's* editorial office on Nassau Street has left a pleasant recollection of his appearance and personality: "He was then what I considered an elderly man,—somewhat over fifty, I imagine,—and was tall or seemed so as he sat at the desk writing, had a pleasant face, a kind, bright eye, and a sweet, gentle voice. . . .The kindness with which Mr. Smith received me removed any apprehension I might have had respecting the treatment I was likely to receive from men of established reputation. . . .Mr. Seba Smith . . . was the first editor, the first poet, and the first man of letters whom I was fortunate enough to meet."[15]

Smith gave up the editorship of *Rover* in January, 1845, and associated himself with a daily paper, the *New York Citizen and American Republican*, a political organ for Native Americanism.[16] After about a year with this paper, he abandoned editorial work until 1852 when he entered the popular field of comic journalism with the *Budget*. Since no copies of the *Budget* have survived, little is known about it except that it sold for fifty cents a year and that it was apparently one of the forty cheap humorous periodicals established between 1850 and 1865, most of which never lived beyond the second year.[17] During the year that the *Budget* lasted, Elizabeth, who was in the West on a lecture tour, sent letters to Seba for publication in the journal.[18] This arrangement is just one of many examples of the ways the family had to work every angle to survive economically.

The Smiths' most ambitious magazine undertaking began in 1854 in association with J. M. Emerson and Company. Mr. Emerson established three periodicals with Smith as their editor: *United States Magazine*, a monthly publication; *United States Journal*, a monthly newspaper; and *United States Weekly Journal*, which reprinted excerpts from the other two. Smith provided good material about a variety of subjects, obtained woodcuts by skilled artists, reprinted some of his Downing letters, and wrote some original satires for these *United States* publications. Then, in 1857, the Emerson Company assumed control of *Putnam's Monthly*, a magazine of high literary quality which had been founded in 1853 as a rival to the prestigious *Harpers's*. Smith assumed editorial supervision of the journal which was then awkwardly titled *Emerson's Magazine and Putnam's Monthly;* and the following January, Smith, in partnership with his wife and sons under the name Oaksmith and Company, bought the magazine. Since the family could not afford to buy writing of the excellence necessary to insure the success of this monthly in a highly competitive market, the publication was suspended in November, 1858.[19]

CHAPTER 7

Poetry and Scholarship

I N January, 1841, when Smith completed the preface to his most serious and lengthy excursion into the field of poetry, he noted that his *Powhatan; A Metrical Romance, in Seven Cantos* represented the work of several years though most of it had been completed during 1840. The two-hundred-page volume, published by Harper & Brothers, appeared two years after the Smiths had settled in New York and the year before Mrs. Smith's tremendously successful long poem *The Sinless Child* was published.

I Powhatan

Powhatan, set in Virginia during 1607 and 1608, deals with the efforts of the Algonquian confederation chief Powhatan to save his people and their land from the English colonists. Though his struggle is foredoomed to failure, his character as leader, father, and human being is portrayed as of untarnished nobility, dauntless courage, heroic pride, and Romantic sensibility. Fierce in battle, too haughty to kneel for the English king, a wily plotter of the destruction of his enemies, Powhatan is nevertheless a true man of feeling whose eyes frequently overflow with sentiment, especially for his youngest daughter, Metoka.

Twelve-year-old Metoka, better known to most readers by the nickname Pocahontas which Seba Smith chooses not to use, is as noble a savage as her father; for she shares his Romantic combination of heroism and compassion. So soft-hearted that she cannot bear to have a hunter kill a deer, she secretly travels by night many miles alone on foot through the forest, and during a howling storm, to warn Sir John [Smith] of an Indian plot to poison the English. The character of Sir John is so little developed[1] that he is merely the object of Powhatan's noble hatred and of Metoka's girlish devotion. The story does not end with Metoka's intervention in Sir John's execution, with her saving of his life, or even with his departure for England. Powhatan remains the center of interest throughout the poem. At the end, having returned from retirement to fight one last battle, he surveys the ruin of his people's greatness; then, with his renowned war club as a staff, he, like Daniel Boone and Huckleberry Finn of later fame, heads toward the West.

Smith's intention in *Powhatan* was to instruct and entertain the common reader; and he sets forth this ideal in the epigraph, the dedication, and the preface to the poem. The epigraph printed on the title page, "He cometh to you with a tale that holdeth children from play and old men from the chimney-corner," is taken from Sir Philip Sidney's *The Defense of Poesy* (1595). Smith is clearly a subscriber to Sidney's doctrine of delightful teaching through literature: "The poet is indeed the right popular philosopher. . . . He cometh to you with words set in delightful proportion, . . . and doth intend the winning of the mind from wickedness to virtue; even as the child is often brought to take most wholesome things, by hiding them in such other as to have a pleasant taste." In a similarly didactic vein, Smith dedicates *Powhatan* "To the Young People of the United States, in the hope that he may do some good in his day and generation, by adding something to the sources of rational enjoyment and mental culture." Elsewhere in the preface, he deprecates poetry that is "too high-flown to be enjoyed and understood by the mass of the reading public" and expresses his preference for the simple excellence that Wordsworth exemplifies in "Lines Written in Early Spring."

Didactic poetry that was intended to have a wide popular appeal was a very old American tradition—one that produced works like Michael Wigglesworth's best-selling theological poem *The Day of Doom: A Poetical Description of the Great and Last Judgment* (1662). Moreover, morally edifying poems about historical subjects were not neglected in the early years. For example, Benjamin Thompson's *New England's Crisis*, a verse account of King Philip's War published in 1676, was a pioneer effort in the tradition which reached its zenith in Longfellow's immensely popular narrative poems with their vivid recital of such classic events in early American history as "Paul Revere's Ride" and "The Courtship of Miles Standish."

The Indians were perennially popular subjects for American literary artists. A scholarly survey has revealed that George Washington and Ulysses S. Grant, the nation's victorious generals in its two most crucial wars and both later Presidents of the republic, have received considerably less attention in American literature as folk heroes than any of a number of Indian chiefs.[2] Noting a particular upsurge of interest in the Indians beginning in the 1830's, Henry Nash Smith has suggested that it may have been a result of Andrew Jackson's harsh treatment of the Indians which caused them to be dramatized as a vanishing race, tragic victims.[3]

The story of Powhatan, Pocahontas, and John Smith has proved particularly attractive to creative writers. There is convincing evidence that Captain Smith himself did the original romanticizing and fictionalizing of the story; for he made himself more heroic, his plight more desperate, and Pocahontas more devoted each time he told the tale. He may, indeed, have invented the whole episode. In any case, later historians picked up the exciting and romantic legend; and it also captured the imaginations of novelists, dramatists, and poets. In 1805, John Davis had dealt with the matter in his novel *First Settlers of Virginia;* Mrs. Lydia Sigourney's *Pocahontas* appeared the same year as Smith's *Powhatan;* and the subject continued to be popular.[4] In fact, as Miss Wyman has demonstrated, Smith's *Powhatan* is in the tradition of American Indian poems that begins with Freneau's "The Indian Student" and "The Indian Burying Ground" and culminates with Longfellow's *Hiawatha* (1855).[5] She notes also the important influence of Sir Walter Scott's metrical romances on Smith and on other authors of American Indian poems.[6]

Smith, who was proud of the historical authenticity of *Powhatan,* asserted in the preface that "it would be difficult to find a poem that embodies more truly the spirit of history, or indeed that follows out more faithfully many of its details." The notes to the poem are formidable: forty-six pages of Indian lore, colonial history, and biography; in addition, numerous footnotes gloss the Indian words in the text and comment about their pronunciation. Smith's zeal for accuracy sometimes leads him into the absurd, as when he solemnly affirms that "The pronunciation [of Opechancanough] adopted in this work throws a slight accent on the first, third, and fifth syllables, which is believed to be more agreeable to the usage of the Indian tribes" (3).

An analysis of the notes reveals that Smith had indeed consulted numerous and reputable authorities that range from John Smith's original *Generall Historie of Virginia* (1624) to Dr. Jedediah Morse's *Report to the Secretary of War of the United States on Indian Af-*

fairs (1822), a work based on firsthand observations under a commission from the President to ascertain the actual state of the Indian tribes.[7] Smith's research into Indian history and lore was so intelligently and thoroughly pursued that it may have started his study of Indian materials that resulted in his publication of a series of articles on "The Religion and Superstitions of the North American Indians" in *The Literary Emporium* for 1846. In the March and April issues, he commented on the beliefs and religious ceremonies of the Chippewas, Sauks, and Musquakies; in May, June, and August, he described beliefs about immortality and ceremonies for the dead among the Hurons, Iroquois, and Chepewyans; in October, he dealt with funeral customs among the West Indian Caraibs and with the religious beliefs of the Senecas.[8]

There is no question that Smith had a perennially popular and potentially excellent subject for a romantic narrative poem or that he prepared himself conscientiously by reading all the best available background materials. Nonetheless, the result was not a successful poem. His shortcomings as a poet became most obvious when he chose a dignified and lofty theme and dared a long, somewhat pretentious project. Considerable internal evidence indicates that Smith originally intended *Powhatan* as an epic. Epic characteristics include the beginning *in medias res*, the largely conceived heroic figure of Powhatan, and long formal speeches followed by such epithetic lines as "Thus spake Pamunky's wily king." The Indians' sacrifices to the gods are reminiscent of scenes from Homer, and a decidedly Miltonic flavor appears in Canto 2, in which the calling of a solemn council of tribal chiefs involves a sonorous listing of names:

> And haste thee to our chieftains all,
> And each unto our council call.
> Call Chesapeakes and Nansamonds,
> And broad Potomoc's warlike sons,
> And rouse the chiefs of every clan,
> From Orapakes to Kecoughtan.

Another Miltonic influence is seen in the description of Powhatan as he presides at the great council. Canto 2, Section 8, begins: "Aloft in stern and regal state/Upon his throne the monarch sate." Smith knew from reading John Smith's *Generall Historie of Virginia* that Powhatan had actually held court sitting on a low bench decorated with raccoon skins, not high on a throne like Milton's Satan, and he would have done better to say so. Another epic analogy may be drawn, this time with *Beowulf*. In the last section of each poem, the hero king is called upon to undertake battle against an enemy of his tribe in his old age. He does not win the fight, but he has great dignity in defeat.[9]

Poe's unkind dismissal of Smith as a writer who did not know "the difference between an epic and an epigram"[10] indicates that Poe believed that Smith had tried to write an epic and had failed. Whether or not such was Smith's original intent, he seems to have realized when the work was finished, that it did not merit the designation of epic: "The author of Powhatan does not presume to claim for his production the merit of good and genuine poetry; nor does he pretend to assign it a place in the classes or forms into which poetry is divided. He has chosen to call it a metrical romance, as a title of less pretension than that of a poem; and he is perfectly willing that others should call it by whatever name they please" (6).

What one must consider *Powhatan* to be is verse characterized by unsureness of taste and technique. The tone ranges from solemn grandeur to maudlin sentimentality. The verse moves most lamely, from the "Proem," done in anapestic tetrameters with many ragged feet, to the patternless juxtaposition of octasyllabic couplets and ballad meter in the cantos. One way of explaining the extraordinary prosody of this work is to speculate that Smith, a college-educated and culturally pretentious literary man—a quoter of Sidney and Wordsworth and a comparer of Homer and Milton—undertook to write in the highest literary tradition; but from time to time as he composed, he unconsciously let his lines fall into the rhythmic and rhyming patterns of English folk poetry. This theory would explain why his couplets suddenly give way to ballad stanzas for no discernible reason and why many of his lines do not scan except by counting (in the old tradition of Anglo-American oral poetry) only the stressed syllables.

Poe's review of *Powhatan* is harsh, derisive in tone, and thoroughly ill-humored. He makes several legitimate objections to the poem when he quotes lines that are mere doggerel and maintains that the great attention to historical accuracy, of which Smith was so proud, is "the leading fault" of the poem. Poe seems principally interested, however, in ridiculing the pretensions of Jack Downing in undertaking a serious poem. Throughout the review he calls Smith by Jack's name, and he concludes that " 'Mr. Downing' never committed a greater mistake in his life than when he fancied himself a poet, even in the ninety-ninth degree." This sort of pretended confusion between Seba Smith and Jack Downing was to occur again and again in criticism of his works. The truth is—though Smith was too modest and too much the gentleman ever to say so—that, whatever their relative merits as poets, Smith had a much surer claim to academic respectability than Poe.

Most reviewers praised *Powhatan*, and some became almost effusive. *Knickerbocker* gave the poem more praise than it deserved.[11] The *Southern Literary Messenger*, unable to say enough good things in one issue, ran a second review three months later to continue the panegyric. "Touching and beautiful in the extreme," the unsigned review calls the poem; and it praises the "musical and appropriate language, . . . always adapted to the subject in hand, stirring or tender as the case may require."[12] "Buy it and read it," is the straightforward advice of another reviewer. "A better 'got up' book never crossed the Atlantic."[13] The *New Yorker* said "We heartily welcome every new attempt to celebrate any portions of the character and scenery of our country or the incidents of her history in either prose or verse; it furnishes foreshadowings of an intellectual and literary Nationality, no less necessary to our perfect independence than distinct forms of political and civil institutions."[14] *Brother Jonathan* (April 24, 1841) offered a most comic and ambiguous kind of compliment. The verse flows smoothly without effort, the reviewer says, except when unpronounceable Indian names are introduced: "In those cases, the rhyme labors like a boa constrictor to gulp down the indigestible, and very well it succeeds too."

Little serious or lasting attention was paid either to *Powhatan* or to Smith's other Indian writings. Rufus W. Griswold praised Elizabeth's appreciation of the "fitness of aboriginal tradition and mythology for the purposes of romantic fiction," but he never mentioned Seba's work on this subject.[15] And it was Elizabeth rather than Seba whom Henry R. Schoolcraft asked to contribute to the chapter on mythology in his *History, Condition, and Prospects of the American Indians*.[16]

II *Popular Poetry*

Though *Powhatan* never brought the acclaim its author had hoped for, some of Smith's less ambitious poetic efforts became very widely known. From his earliest attempts, he had a sure touch for appealing to the popular taste with his sentimental, melodramatic, or comic newspaper poetry. His verses were picked up by other papers and widely reprinted, often without the author's name; and, as has been mentioned, the compilers of giftbooks and literary annuals found his work ideally suited to the tastes of their readers. His poems were published in school books where they were read by generation after generation of children and committed to memory for recitation at Friday afternoon elocution sessions. Indeed, some of Smith's poems achieved the ultimate in a certain ironic kind of immortality when they became so widely reprinted, so well-known in recitation or song, that they passed into the oral tradition of anonymous literature and eventually became a part of American folklore. His verses fit easily into the old traditional English ballad tunes.

As has already been noted, *Powhatan*, a work growing out of the study and imitation of literary models, sometimes lapses into the old rhythms of English folk poetry. Conversely, there are literary influences and echoes in Smith's folk-type poems. Two traditions are clearly represented in his poetry, as in all his thought and writing: the academic tradition and the folk tradition. He was a Phi Beta Kappa graduate of Bowdoin, and he was a student of Homer and Milton. He was also the descendant of a lively New England tradition of folk poetry, for his family boasted several untrained poets: his grandmother, Anna Crossman Smith was considered to have a gift as a versifier; and his Uncle Jasiel, who had built a log cabin next to Seba's father's in Buckfield, wrote songs and composed rhymed epitaphs for gravestones in the village cemetery.[17]

In 1867 Smith recalled, "For twenty or thirty years I have somewhat frequently encountered persons who, happening to discover the authorship and ownership of some early waif [of mine] expressed much gratification at the discovery, saying it had been familiar to them from childhood, and they had heard children repeating it in the street in distant cities."[18] The comic poems of Smith's which were best known in this fashion were "Sam Patch" and "Old Bachelors at Auction."[19] The most widely circulated of the tearful, sentimental verses were "The Mother Perishing in the Snow Storm," "Three Little Graves," and "Fair Charlotte."

Smith's earliest popular success as a writer came from "The Mother Perishing in the Snow Storm," which he published in the *Eastern Argus* during his first year out of college. This shameless tear-jerker, based on a true local incident in which a woman wrapped all her warm clothing about her baby when lost on an icy winter night, was reprinted widely, was translated into foreign languages, was included in many school readers, was set to music, and was popular a quarter of a century later on the concert stage as sung by the Hutchinson family singers.[20]

Smith's "Three Little Graves" was given particular notice by a reviewer of *Bowdoin Poets*, an 1841 anthology: "The following little poem, which we extract from the book for its great simplicity and pathos, may be familiar to some of our readers, for it went the rounds of the newspapers several years ago; and though anonymous, has found its way into several school-books and compilations of American poetry. The author's name has never been connected with it till it appeared in this volume of the Bowdoin Poets."[21] The admiring reviewer then quotes all seventeen stanzas of Smith's poem, which presents a child's view of death and is clearly derivative of William Wordsworth's "We Are Seven." A boy, whose little sister has died and been buried, asks:

> "Mama, why can't we take her up,
> "And put her in my bed!
> "I'll feed her from my little cup,
> "And then she won't be dead."

The best known of all Smith's verses is, however, "Fair Charlotte." Based on a story in the *New York Observer* of February 8, 1840, the ballad stanza narrative relates the tragic end of a vain young girl who went to a dance on a bitter cold New Year's Eve:

> "Now daughter dear," her mother cried,
> "This blanket round you fold,
> "For 'tis a dreadful night abroad,
> "You'll catch your death a-cold."
>
> "O nay, O nay," fair Charlotte said,
> And she laugh'd like a gypsy queen,
> "To ride with blankets muffled up,
> "I never could be seen."

When the sleigh reaches the village inn, her sweetheart discovers that "His Charlotte was a stiffen'd corpse,/And word spake never more!"[22]

When Smith published this ballad as "A Corpse Going to a Ball" in *Rover* on December 28, 1843, he perhaps did so as a timely warning to girls to dress warmly for the holiday festivities. Immediately picked up for reprinting, the poem soon passed into the oral tradition as a song; and Smith's authorship was forgotten. In the process of oral transmission, the usual changes were made in the original text: several moralizing stanzas were tacked onto the end, the puzzling "gypsy queen" became a hardly more satisfactory "gypsum queen," and other minor variations were introduced. The song, known now usually as "Fair Charlotte," "Young Charlotte," or "The Frozen Girl," spread even into regions of the South where snow and bitterly cold winters are hardly known; and it was carried into the Midwest, probably by blind Mormon folksinger William l. Carter. Folklorist Harold W. Thompson, writing in 1939, called it "one of our most popular ballads" and ranked it as "one of the three or four most popular in Northeastern New York." Alan Lomax in his scholarly study of *The Folk Songs of North America* (1960), says this is "one ballad almost certain to be encountered by the collector in any part of the country a few years ago." In 1934 Phillips Barry traced "Fair Charlotte" back to the pen of Seba Smith, but it is still widely sung in the folk tradition and continues to be anthologized sometimes as among those ballads "whose authors are lost in antiquity."[23]

It is easy to see why "Fair Charlotte" fooled the folklorists for so many years. Most authentic folk ballads from Maine record actual or reputed happenings, many are connected with death by freezing, and most end with a moral message. An example is "The Mark Bachelder Tragedy" which ends:

> They dragged his lifeless form away,
> And quickly put him in his sleigh;
> Started his horse and sent him home,
> There to freeze and die alone.
>
> And now young men and maidens all,
> Take warning thus by me;
> And e'er abide on virtue's side,
> And shun bad company.[24]

Although the content, tone, metrical structure, and style of "Fair Charlotte" are very close to those of New England folk ballads, the literary scholar notes a suspicious echoing of Wordsworth's Lucy Poems in the first quatrain:

> Young Charlotte lived by the mountain side,
> A wild and lonely spot;
> No dwelling there, for three miles round,
> Except her father's cot.

An obvious question today is why such mediocre poems as "The Mother Perishing in a Snow Storm," "Three Little Graves," and "Fair Charlotte" enjoyed such wide and long popularity. The temptation to psychoanalyze Smith and his audience is irresistible; and Lomax, who has made a gesture in that direction, has remarked that there is a touch of the erotic in Charlotte's bare-shouldered, unchaperoned ride and that the conclusion is pleasantly morbid. He notes Poe's successful exploitation of materials "similar and only slightly more sophisticated."[25] There is eroticism too in the perishing mother poem, for the heroine removes so much of her clothing in order to wrap the baby that she is found with her bare breast frozen as cold and hard as marble.

Leslie Fiedler, who has pushed such speculation about as far as it can be pushed, dwells at length on the age's preoccupation with dead ladies. "To save the female for polite readers who wanted women but not sex was not an easy matter," Fiedler says. "The only safe woman is a dead woman; but even she, if young and beautiful, is only half safe, as any American knows, recalling the necrophilia of Edgar Allan Poe. The only *safe*, safe female is a pre-adolescent girl dying or dead."[26] As for the little dead sister in "Three Little Graves," it may be far fetched to find suggestions of necrophilia and incest in the boy's desire to take his sister's corpse into his bed; but, as Fiedler puts it, "it is perhaps the fault of our post-Freudian imaginations, incapable of responding sentimentally rather than analytically to such images."[27] Of course, on the surface all three poems were models of propriety; they told very moral stories; and the erotic elements were on a level that the genteel reader did not have to recognize with his conscious mind. No wonder such poems were popular.

Smith's feeling about these popular poems was ambiguous. He cannot have taken them very seriously at the time of composition, he knew they deserved no significant place in literature, but he was understandably sorry later not to have the credit for work so widely known and admired. Putting his papers in order the year before his death, he gathered these fugitive items together in a notebook, entitled the never published collection "Scattered Waifs of Fifty

Years," and wrote a brief and modest introduction in which he said in part:

"Of making many books there is no end." I do not therefore ask the book-burdened world to read this little volume, nor critics to sit in judgment upon it. The latter have enough to do to look after volumes of more pretensions. . . . Having passed the allotted age of man, I feel but little solicitude about the popular success of this little volume. I know there are a few who will cherish it, as they love and will cherish the memory of the author.[28]

III New Elements of Geometry

Although Smith took himself seriously as a poet only part of the time, he always took himself seriously as a scholar, with sometimes unhappy consequences. One brief, tragicomic episode in his career as an author concerns *New Elements of Geometry*. He was, by his own account, a self-taught mathematical amateur whose attention was casually drawn to some classical problems of mathematics such as doubling the volume of a cube and solving equations of the fifth degree. He devoted three years of intense study to these matters, and in 1850 published in his book a theory based on the idea that "the roots in mathematics are essentially and necessarily expressions of geometrical forms, the square root necessarily representing the side of a square in form, and the cube root representing the linear edge of a cube in form,"[29] a philosophy obviously derived from earlier geometers. He argues for considering geometry as a concrete and mechanical rather than as an abstract science. Theorizing that lines and surfaces have thickness, he arrives at the conclusion that all measurements should be computed on a cubic basis.

Smith's hopes for *New Elements of Geometry* were very high. Believing this work to be "the most important labor of his life," he devoted half the pages of his autobiography to an exposition of its ideas. In this treatise, he stated, "there are things that the world will not let die, though it may be slow to receive them."[30] In his eagerness to make known what he thought to be important scientific discoveries, Smith sent copies of the book to Auguste Comte, to the Smithsonian Institution, and to at least eighteen presidents and professors of mathematics at Ivy League colleges. He offered to present illustrated lectures about his ideas at the various campuses and did give some such addresses. But the response was not what he had hoped for. Most scholars ignored his letters or sent polite noncommittal replies, but some became annoyed by his combination of ignorance, enthusiasm, and persistence. Comte, in response to Smith's second letter, was severely critical of the volume and urged that no second edition be issued.[31] Smith wrote to a friend in 1851 that Professor Pierce of Harvard "a few days ago utterly refused *to have any conversation* with me on the subject."[32]

Having little formal training in mathematics, Smith was fascinated by the notion of solving scientific problems by the application of common sense. Significantly, he was much impressed by the efforts of John A. Parker of New York to square the circle by principles "drawn from nature, which are plain and simple, as all the works of nature are when we once get at them."[33] Unfortunately, simple, natural insights are inadequate for scientific inquiry.

A Columbia University mathematician, criticizing Smith's work about 1925, noted absurdities in the book and denied the ideas any validity or significance; but he stated that "the crude work . . . shows some native ingenuity."[34] Scholars of our own day, who continue to take a dim view of Smith's contribution to the science of mathematics, are exemplified by Professor Duane Darrel Blumberg:

> Smith's work is flawed by error and also reveals his ignorance of the mathematics of his day. For example he asserts incorrectly that "the first four powers of all numbers or quantities always have perfect roots, either square or cube, or both, . . . but the fifth power of any number or quantity never in any case has a perfect root, either square or cube." He then goes on to state his belief that this is the reason for the unsolvability of the general quintic equation by radicals. However, Abel had given a complete analysis of the quintic equation in 1824 and Galois' brilliant work on the solvability of the general equation had been done prior to 1832.[35]

Smith lived before the era of specialization, when any educated person still felt free to speculate about problems of intellectual interest, even if they were "out of his field." It was his insistence on recognition from the academic authorities that brought his work so many rebuffs. Despite his perceptiveness about Jack Downing's unfitness for high public office, Smith could not see that he himself was equally unsuited to debate questions of higher mathematics with trained scholars, and he made himself as ludicrous in their eyes as Jack was in his own. Smith in the world of science, like Jack in the world of national and international politics, was equipped with no more than "some native ingenuity" and with too much ambitious self-confidence.

CHAPTER 8

May-Day in New York

S EBA Smith's 1845 resurrection of Jack Downing in *May-Day in New-York; or, House-Hunting and Moving*, resulted in a mixed bag of material. Although Smith's name does not appear on the title page, internal evidence indicates the work is all his. A twenty-eight page "Preface by the Publishers" outlines a comic history of "Downing Literature." Probably written by Smith, the mock literary history devotes several paragraphs to the limitations of Charles Augustus Davis, a New York "city-bred silk-stocking."[1] According to the account, literary ambition and a passion for popularity motivated Davis' theft of the character of Jack Downing. Smith deflates Davis' pretentions to the laurels of literature by never mentioning his name; instead, he refers to him as a "respectable merchant," "a heavy iron dealer," "the Broad street merchant," and "the merchant"—by implication, Davis is neither a gentleman nor a man of letters. In fact, Davis had by this time abandoned writing. A friend of Nicholas Biddle, long president of the Bank of the United States, Davis had appropriated the character of Jack merely as a convenient mask for satire; once Jackson had destroyed the bank, Davis ceased to write. The preface concludes with accounts of other shoots from the root of Downing literature: Jack's popularity in the graphic arts and his influence on such figures as Thomas Chandler Haliburton's Sam Slick.

I *Jack Attacked and Defended*

The closing portion of the little volume includes three sketches under Seba Smith's own name (discussed below as part of '*Way Down East*, Chapter 1) and a Postcript that defends Jack Downing against a heavy lament by *The American Review* (June, 1845). That worthy journal, desiring a national literature, observed that the only American school of writers produced mere Jack Downings and Sam

Slicks—characters who served only to "degrade and vulgarise the tongue and the taste of the country." Smith's reply, selected friendly reviews from newspapers, shows that he took satisfaction in having his work recognized as an early sign of America's "intellectual independence" and in reviewers' perception of the letters as "graphic," "piquant, racy, and original." He reprinted reviews which praised his work as faithful to "Yankee peculiarities" and admired his language as "the richest and most natural Yankee dialect"—perceptive evaluations.

II   *May Day Moving*

The central portion of the book, Jack's account of the traditional moving day in the city of New York, that he offered in three letters to his Aunt Keziah, has folkloric significance. The title of the volume and the central idea of the epistolary section come from a custom which probably astonished Smith as much when he moved to New York City in 1839 as it reportedly had Davy Crockett when he had visited the place five years earlier. According to *An Account of Col. Crockett's Tour to The North and Down East:*

Next morning, being the first of May, . . . we drove up the city, and took a view of the improvements and beautiful houses in the new part. By the time we returned down Broadway, it seemed to me that the city was flying before some awful calamity. "Why," said I, "colonel, what under heaven is the matter? Everybody appears to be pitching out their furniture and packing it off." He laughed, and said this was the general "mooving day." Such a sight nobody ever saw, unless it was in this same city. It seemed a kind of frolic, as if they were changing houses just for fun. Every street was crowded with carts, drays, and people.[2]

Moving to the slum section called Five Points, Crockett was amazed to see people burning their straw beds in the streets, black and white citizens sharing jugs of liquor, "and such fidling and dancing nobody ever saw before in this world." Mulling over the scene, he concluded: "I do think I saw more drunk folks, men and women, that day, than I ever saw before."[3]

Both Davy Crockett and Jack Downing in their accounts of May Day moving emphasize the enormous confusion, inevitable when all the poor people in a big city try to move at the same time. Each writer notes the element of renewal suggested by the burning of old beds and by the breaking of crockery. The atmosphere of crude festival abroad in the streets is developed by Crockett in his emphasis on drinking and dancing and by Jack in his presentation of rude repartee between young men and girls. The participation of men and women, whites and blacks, in the festivities emphasizes the mood of saturnalia or carnival, the aspect which doubtless accounts for the survival of a folkway preserved in defiance of all reason and order. Like the Indian custom of the busk—an annual burning of old possessions—which Thoreau so much admired, it was impractical from a materialistic point of view but refreshing to the spirit.[4]

A general moving day sometime in May was a custom brought to America by immigrants from the British Isles, particularly from Scotland, where "Whitsunday term" (formerly May 15; later, May 26 or 28) was known, at least well into the nineteenth century, as "flitting day." The origin of this legal date for renewing contracts is connected ultimately with Pentecost as the festival of the inauguration of the New Covenant of Christianity. The ecclesiastical association of the date is lost in America, but several elements of the Old World custom survive. Jack mentions that the day for giving notice of moving is February 2, a date which preserves the tradition of giving such notice on Candlemas, the Feast of the Purification, and again suggests the ceremonial element of spring renewal. In the New World as in the Old, the hour of noon marks the moment when all leases end. And descriptions of the old Scottish "flitting day" emphasize the same wild atmosphere: teeming, chaotic streets; excited, rushing people; broken and lost possessions; and a general air "more confused and savage than the roughest picnic."[5] The word "picnic" suggests Crockett's "frolic," and both parallel the tone of Jack's attempt to convey the mood of the day to Aunt Keziah: "Oh, of all the days in my life-time—I've seen trainin' days, and muster days, and independent days, and . . . Christmas and New-Year's days; but of all the days that ever I did see in this 'ere world, moving-day in New-York is the cap-sheaf" (43).

Since moving day is an urban custom, it is foreign to both Davy Crockett and Jack Downing, who idealize the rustic stability of a life close to nature. For Crockett, this better way of life is epitomized by that honored American frontier institution, the log cabin; for Smith, by the gathering of wild flowers on May Day, a folk custom that predates urban development and harks back to the most ancient pagan fertility rites of spring.[6] "It would take a good deal to get me out of my log house," Crockett remarks, "but here, I understand,

many persons 'moove' every year." And Smith has Jack contrast the
May Days in New York to those in Downingville:

It is no more like the May-days we used to have in Downingville, than a
toad under a harrow is like a man on horseback. You know what good, pleasant times we used to have when the first of May come round in Downingville, how everything in the house was all slicked up a day or two
beforehand as neat as a pin, and the things in every room all sot to rights,
and the children's faces all washed, and their heads combed, and their
clean clothes all ready for em to put on. And then, about sunrise May morning, what a scampering there was among the children! They'd come dart-
ing out of all the houses like flocks of new butterflies, all dressed up as neat
as pinks, and their eyes glistening and shining like glass buttons. And away
they'd fly in whole swarms across the fields, and up the hills, and away in
the woods; and when they come back to breakfast you couldn't tell which
was the reddest, their cheeks or the bunches of flowers they had in their
hands. And every part of Downingville all day would smell as sweet as a
rose.
    But 'taint so in New-York, aunt Keziah, not by a jug-full." (43)

In these letters Jack is cast in an unfamiliar role: he is neither an
observer of politics nor a bumptious rustic in the city; he appears to
be living in a poor section of New York, to be married and the
father of two, and to have other relatives crowded into his third-
story rooms. Jack details his bewilderment at and his eventual adjustment to the May Day rental customs. Pressed by the new ways,
by demanding landlords, and by violently aggressive neighbors—feeling perhaps like the toad under the harrow in his
metaphor—Jack finds himself evicted from his old apartment and
settled in a new one under difficulties more painful than comic. He
himself is bullied, his wife and children are abused to tears, and the
new home is found after great effort, at the last minute, and at the
cost of broken dishes and furniture—in addition to the distress of
his family. The ugly buildings, the threateningly crowded streets,
the verminous mattress-straw fires, and the gross people create a
Dickensian oppression that is only increased by the mood of
grotesque revelry. Jack's familial responsibilities weigh on him, and
he acts with considerably less exuberant freedom and self-assurance
than the character of the 1833 letters. Smith did not revive the May-
Day letters for his 1859 collection of Jack's writings.

CHAPTER 9

'Way Down East

E ARLY in 1854, when Smith wrote to Mr. N. Cleveland of Brooklyn, he was apparently answering a request for information about Bowdoin graduates. He provided a few anecdotes—mostly uncharitable—about his former classmates and spoke modestly of his own achievements. Conceding that the Jack Downing letters had enjoyed "very great popularity," he insisted that they were, nevertheless, of little "intrinsic merit." Summarizing his career as a writer, Smith said: "I have published but one volume that I think of much account, and that is the 'New Elements of Geometry.' Most of my other writings consist of fugitive articles in prose and verse, which have appeared in periodicals, but have not been collected in volumes; though some of them perhaps may be at no very distant day."[1] The book Smith indicated as under preparation was undoubtedly 'Way Down East; or, Portraitures of Yankee Life, which was published later in the same year by Derby and Jackson of New York. At least three other editions of 'Way Down East appeared in 1854 in Boston, Philadelphia, and Cincinnati; and later editions appeared in the same cities in 1855, 1857, 1859, 1860, 1866, 1876, and 1884.[2] In Miss Wyman's judgment, one in which most critics would concur, 'Way Down East is, next to the Downing letters, the most valuable and popular of Smith's works.[3]

I Organizational Problems

As Smith remarked, many of the sketches had previously appeared in periodicals. These included some of the more respectable journals of the day: the Knickerbocker, the Ladies' Companion, Burton's Magazine, Godey's Lady's Book, as well as Smith's own short-lived venture, Rover. Another group of the 'Way Down East stories had already been included in Smith's 1845 collection, May-Day in New York; or, House-Hunting and Moving; Illustrated

and Explained in Letters to Aunt Keziah. By Major Jack Downing.
This title was descriptive of only the first half of the volume; for the
concluding section, entitled "Sketches from Life," was ascribed to
Seba Smith and was labeled as "inserted at the special request of
Major Downing." The *May-Day* sketches reprinted in *'Way Down
East* were "Perseverance: or Peter Punctual's Way to Collect Bills,"
entitled "Peter Punctual" in *'Way Down East;* "Polly Gray and the
Doctors," with the title unchanged; and "Christopher Crotchet:
The Singing Master," which became simply "Christopher
Crotchet." Smith made no significant revisions in these sketches for
their republication.

In spite of the distinction made in *May-Day in New-York*
between Major Downing, the author of letters to Aunt Keziah, and
Seba Smith, the writer of "stories and sketches of humor" (71), the
'Way Down East volume was persistently associated with Jack
Downing. The title page reads "by Seba Smith/ the/ original Major
Jack Downing," but at least some editions had only "Jack Dow-
ning" on the spine. Reviewers tended to attribute the sketches to
Jack, but not one of the stories is presented in the epistolary form or
is written as if by Jack. The reviewer for *Putnam's* acknowledges the
strange relationship between Jack and Seba by referring to Jack as
Seba's "straw auxiliary, or rather *doppelganger.*"[4] To the *Harper's*
reviewer, Jack has completely absorbed Seba's personality:

> The veritable Jack Downing again makes his appearance in these
> genuine specimens of the comic traits in New England character. No man is
> more completely at home in this kind of delineation than the worthy Major.
> His keen perception of humor is matched only by his skill in life-like por-
> traitures. His brain is over-flowing with Yankee traditions, local anecdotes,
> and personal recollections, which he reproduces with a freshness and point
> which always protects the reader from satiety. The force of his descriptions
> consists in their perfect naturalness. They are never over-charged—never
> distorted, for the sake of grotesque effect—never spiced too highly for the
> healthy palate.[5]

It is not enough that the simple country boy, Jack, has become Major Downing, friend and adviser to presidents; he is also acclaimed
as a deft literary artist who has a sure touch for local-color writing of
a genteel sort.

Another misleading quality of the critical comments about *'Way
Down East* is illustrated in the *Harper's* review in which the

sketches are called "genuine specimens of the comic traits of New England character." Smith himself seems to have thought of the book in this vein; for, in his autobiography, written May 7, 1858, he referred to the collection as "an illustrated volume of his humorous stories."[6] In his prefatory remarks to the second part of *May-Day in New-York*, he calls the narratives "stories and sketches of humor" (71). In fact, not even half of the sixteen chapters in the book are humorous, either in the sense of comic or in the older meaning of humor—dealing with eccentricities of character. Moreover, not all the chapters have down East or even New England settings and characters.

Though Smith called the sketches "chapters," suggesting the work as one artistic unit, there is no unifying theme or structure to the book. Simply a collection of various kinds of narratives, this work is arranged according to no detectable plan, and not only the kind but the quality of the writing varies widely. At the worst, some of the 'Way Down East stories are embarrassingly poor; but the best of them, lovingly detailed and quietly humorous vignettes of life in or near New England, are good early examples of the genre which later was called "local color."

II   The Puritan Past

The first sketch, "John Wadleigh's Trial," is a product of Smith's taste for regional antiquarianism, a pursuit he relished as much as his more illustrious New England contemporaries Hawthorne and Thoreau. His interest in early Americana had already been demonstrated in *Powhatan*; in "Gleanings from Early New England History," a collection of odd and interesting bits of information learned from oral tradition, old letters, and wills;[7] and in "The General Court and Jane Andrews' Firkin of Butter," based on a 1640 legal proceeding.[8] "John Wadleigh's Trial" is based on information searched out in seventeenth- and eighteenth-century court records from New Hampshire and the Province of Maine. Never penetrating beneath a good-humored, superficial analysis of Puritan mores, the sketch examines judicial proceedings against offenders of Puritan decorum, particularly the unfortunate John Wadleigh who is charged with sleeping in church. Where Hawthorne found the stuff of tragedy, and where Thoreau discovered material for serious contemplation of the human condition, Smith unearthed merely quaint eccentricities and genial comedy.

Nonetheless, Smith's sketch is not without interest. Smith's portrait of the judge, presiding with an over-full belly, puffing at a
pipe, sitting at ease with his feet on the table, recalls Washington Irving's reductive sketches of colonial New York worthies in the
Knickerbocker history. The language is skillfully employed, especially the contrast between the attorneys' flowery elegance of address and the witnesses' homely simplicity. "What is the state of
your hearing?" a lawyer asks. "Sharp as a needle with two pints,"
replies a witness (23). Lawyer Chandler addresses the court in
mock-heroic strains:

"May it please your honor, I am astonished, I am amazed at the hardihood
and effrontery of my learned friend. . . . Why, sir, if there ever was a case
made out in any court under heaven, by clear, positive, and irresistible
evidence, it is this. Sir, I say, sir, evidence as clear as sunshine and irresistible as thunder. . . . And when posterity shall see the account of this trial,
should the culprit go clear, they may cry out 'judgment has fled to brutish
beasts and men have lost their reason'; but they shall not say Chandler did
not do his duty." (25 - 27)

To this one may compare a witness's account of what he has observed of Wadleigh's conduct during long sermons: " 'I've generally
noticed if he begins to gape at seventhly and eighthly, it's gone
goose with him before he gets through tenthly, and he has to look
out for another prop to his head somewhere, for his neck isn't stiff
enough to hold it up. And from tenthly up to sixteenthly, he's dead
as a door nail; till the Amen brings the people up to prayers, and
then Wadleigh comes up with a jerk, jest like opening a jack-
knife' " (21).[9] This homely speech is written without condescension,
for the forthright witness with his folk metaphors and rustic dialect
and even poor drowsy John Wadleigh are not ridiculous. Instead,
the formal institutions and authority figures of the community are
satirized: the foolish judge, the pompous lawyers, the long-winded
preacher, and the whole comic spectacle of a solemn court hearing
on a trivial matter.

"John Wadleigh's Trial" includes a number of traditional
elements that are drawn as much from New England folklore as
from historical records. The Yankee's inability to give a direct
answer to a simple question is proverbial, as noted by Richard M.
Dorson in his study of New England popular tales and legends.[10]
Smith illustrates this character trait in the scene in the courtroom in
which the witness is asked, "*What* do you know about John

Wadleigh's sleeping in meeting?" and replies, "I know *all* about it.
I guess 'taint no secret" (19). When the lawyer presses him for a
plain answer, the witness responds with a long account about how
warm it gets in church, about what a hard-working man Wadleigh
is, and about how long and "heavy-like" Parson Moody's sermons
are. Parson Moody, the Reverend Samuel Moody of York, Maine,
was an eccentric gentleman who was celebrated in folktales that
succeeding generations of New Englanders loved to hear and tell.
Since humorous anecdotes about him are included in several local
publications,[11] Smith may have obtained his information about
Moody from printed or oral sources, or from both. Certainly the
name of the legendary Parson Moody would have been enough to
provoke a smile from his readers.
     The crime of which Wadleigh was accused was the subject of
numerous anecdotes and of traditional beliefs and customs. In
Treasury of New England Folklore, Benjamin A. Botkin prints five
anecdotes about peoples' sleeping in church, three from early
farmers' almanacs and two from oral traditions recorded in the
manuscript collections of the Federal Writers' Projects for the states
of Maine and New Hampshire. Botkin also cites old histories and
reminiscences which record the devices ministers used to keep people awake or to wake them up and of the custom of carrying sprigs
of caraway, dill, or coriander to church meetings and of nibbling
them when drowsiness threatened.[12] Smith was working within a
traditional body of New England folklore, familiar both to him and
to many of his readers, which was a common source for popular
humorous stories.
     Perhaps the many traditional motifs "John Wadleigh's Trial" in-
cluded helped to make it popular. On March 25, 1847, the *Yankeee
Blade*, a Boston journal, reprinted the sketch from Smith's original
magazine publication, with this headnote: "A droll story of the
Puritan Times in New England, by Seba Smith, is going the rounds
of the press from Calais to Matamoros. It was originally for the N.Y.
Illustrated Magazine." Though the story may not have reached
quite to Calais or to Matamoros, it did reach the pages of the New
York *Spirit of the Times*, the best known and the most influential of
all the sporting and humor journals, where, on July 10, 1847, the
scene where the witness gives his testimony was reprinted.[13]
     In "Seating the Parish," another historical sketch that is based on
old records, Smith tells of a settlement of Boston Puritans on Long
Island in 1655 and of the movement of this small community away

from primitive simplicity and pure democracy until the time when, corrupted by prosperity, the congregation refurbishes the old church, builds pews to replace the original plank benches, and institutes a caste system of apportioning pews. "Seating the Parish" had originally been published in May, 1843, in the *Ladies' Companion*, a New York imitator of Philadelphia's *Godey's* and *Graham's*, which had already published many of Elizabeth's efforts and several of Seba's. Much less lively than "John Wadleigh's Trial," this sketch is the sort of work which prompted Charles Lanman, a critic of the *Ladies' Companion*, to call the journal "a milk-and-water concern." [14]

The fifteenth chapter, "Old Meyers," also a historical sketch, treats romantically a semilegendary old frontiersman of the Daniel Boone sort who moved ever farther westward before other settlers and who was last heard of in 1838 when he decided that Illinois was becoming too populous. Smith describes how Old Meyers girded on his tomahawk and scalping knife; took down the dried remains of his panther's head from the wall of the cabin; gave one last, loud, shrill whoop; and "then Old Meyers, the Panther, turned his face to the westward, and took up his solitary march for the distant wilderness" (369). Here, as in the ending of *Powhatan*, Smith evokes the powerful symbolic connotations of the West and the wilderness.

III   *Three Moral Tracts*

All the *'Way Down East* stories, except the historical anecdotes already discussed, have some sort of plot development. A reviewer for *Putnam's* said of the sketches: "Several of them are funny and spirited. . . . The remainder are respectable," and he added that some have "the peculiarity of tapering off in a disappointing manner, without any perceptible catastrophe." [15] The merely "respectable" stories are "Peter Punctual," "Billy Snub," and "Jerry Guttridge"—all solemn moral tales designed to inculcate a Franklinesque set of values. Peter demonstrates the virtue of financial responsibility in a very dull manner; Billy illustrates at tedious length how sobriety, industry, and frugality are rewarded; and the tale about Jerry dramatizes the reformation of an irresponsible idler by upright neighbors who, to his everlasting moral regeneration, have him sentenced to a public whipping.

These three depressing tales are little more than tracts that seem out of place in the otherwise entertaining and good-humored volume. Yet Smith obviously thought well of them, for he had published two of them before, "Peter Punctual" in 1845 in *May-Day in New-York* and "Jerry Guttridge'" six years earlier in the *Knickerbocker*.[16]

IV   *Rural New England*

The remaining stories, though some indeed do taper off "without any perceptible catastrophe," are all lively sketches of New England rustic life in the Golden Age of the not too distant past. They are filled richly with the folklore and folkways of early nineteenth-century, down East life: games, amusements, sports, courting customs, treasure lore, witch and devil lore, superstitions, traditional foods and drinks, festivals, pranks, and tall tales. And they convey a strong sense of community among New Englanders who stand together against a hostile environment and trouble-making strangers and who do not just survive grimly but take an earthy satisfaction in whatever simple good times they can manage.

Smith's vision of family and village life emphasizes affection, even indulgence of spouses and children; a willingness to play as well as work; and generosity to neighbors—all useful correctives to the stereotype of the Yankee as stingy, shifty, and sly—as possessed by a wholly materialistic set of values. The contrast may be clearly shown by the following examples. Dorson cites several anecdotes that illustrate the traditional attitude that "New England parsimony did not retreat for death": "Yankee materialism comes to the fore in 'The Last Wrong,' where Liza refuses dying Hiram a piece of ham because she plans to serve it at his funeral. A kindred Maine farmer registered regret when his wife hung herself in an apple tree, because she kicked off so many green apples."[17]

Botkin illustrates the point that "to waste either time or money was to a Yankee the breaking of the Ten Commandments" with the following anecdote: "When a good old deacon had passed away, his relict, waiting in the darkened room for the funeral to begin, whispered to her daughter, 'Hand me my knitting. I might knit a few bouts while the folks are gathering.'" Botkin not only reports the story of the parsimonious widower who breaks his wife's tombstone to patch the oven and whose biscuits come to the table imprinted with the words "Sacred to the memory of my beloved wife Mathilda," but also includes a story called "The Secret of True

Economy": "Two men met on the street one day, and in the course
of conversation the one said to the other: 'How do you manage to
feed your large family on your small income?' 'Well,' he responded,
'I'll tell you. I find out what they don't like and give 'em plenty of
it.' "[18] Smith was surely acquainted with the stereotypes indicated
by such anecdotes, but they did not embody his vision of the
Yankee character.

One may consider, for example, the behavior of the Frier family
in "Jerry Guttridge." On learning that neighbors are in need, the
Friers make up a basket of bread, milk, meat, and vegetables for
them. Then they decide to add a pie, "so the poor starving cre'turs
might have a little taste of something that was good" (134). This
adding of a touch of human kindness to what might be required as a
Christian's duty is typical of Smith's Yankees. In the same story,
Mr. Frier, who is very much concerned about getting in his hay
before a rain storm, ends by letting three of the four tons of hay be
ruined while he tries to help Mrs. Guttridge and her children. The
following discussions of other sketches from 'Way Down East indicate that incidents of unselfishness, generosity, and affection are
frequent in Smith's "portraitures of Yankee life."

V   Dying in New England

"Seth Woodsum's Wife" and "Polly Gray and the Doctors" are
among the stories praised by the reviewer for Putnam's as "funny
and spirited." They are not only refreshingly free of the sentimentality which often weakened Smith's work but also have more fully
developed plots than most of the sketches. Both stories involve the
illness and one the death of a woman, the era's favorite excuses for
emotional extravagance in literature. But Smith provides a welcome
surprise: he treats both episodes as comedy.

"Seth Woodsum's Wife," which was first published in Godey's
Lady's Book in February, 1840, as "Cure of a Hypochondriac,"
begins as Seth Woodsum is mowing one morning in his hayfield
when his little daughter comes running from the house to report
that "Mother is dreadful sick; she's on the bed, and says she shall
die before you get there" (370). Having "a tender attachment for
his wife" (370), Seth drops his scythe, runs to the house, hastens to
the bedside, takes his wife's hand, comforts her as best he can, and
sends for the doctor. When the doctor arrives, he finds nothing
physically wrong with Mrs. Woodsum. He gives her some harmless

medicine and advises Seth to keep her cheerful and busy and tells him she will be all right. Before long, however, she has another attack of the same hypochondria. Seth leaves his plough in mid-furrow and rushes to her side. The attacks recur repeatedly week after week and month after month, each seeming more severe than the last; and Mrs. Woodsum becomes convinced that she soon must die. She begs her husband to remarry when she goes, so the children shall have a mother. Unfailing in patience and affection, he assures her that death will not dissolve the holy bond that unites them.

At last, however, Seth comes to believe that it will give his wife mental tranquility if he agrees to remarry. The next time she is stricken and begs him to promise to do so, he says with a sigh, "Well, then, if you insist on it, my dear—I have thought if it should be the will of Providence to take you from us to be here no more, I have thought I should marry for my second wife, Hannah Lovejoy." Thereupon Mrs. Woodsum leaps "from the bed like a cat." "What! Hannah Lovejoy to be the mother of my children! No, that's what she never shall. So you may go to your ploughing, Mr. Woodsum, and set your heart at rest" (384). She never becomes ill again.

"Polly Gray and the Doctors," reprinted from *May-Day in New-York* (85 - 102), begins with a scene of family consternation over the sudden, mysterious, and severe illness of Polly, the young daughter, a situation which Smith handles with humor rather than sentimentality. Deacon Gray refuses to heed his wife's impassioned pleas that he send for the doctor, for he believes that Polly is just romantically interested in the young physician. Throughout Mrs. Gray's hysterical urgings that Polly is at death's door, he proceeds methodically to unload the wagon, turn the horse into the pasture, pet the dog, and change into dry clothes. Then, when he discovers the gravity of Polly's condition, he demands to know why he wasn't told how sick she was when he first got home.

When Dr. Longley arrives, he has two comic conversations, one with Mrs. Gray and the other with a neighbor woman, Mrs. Livermore. When he asks Mrs. Gray what she has given Polly, she replies, "Nothing, but arb-drink; whenever she felt worse, I made her take a good deal of arb-drink, because that, you know, is always good, doctor. And besides, when it can't do no good, it would do no hurt" (103). On the doctor's inquiry about what kind of herb-drink she had administered, Mrs. Gray recalls, "Well, I give her most all sorts, for we had a plenty of 'em in the house. I give her sage, and peppermint, and sparement, and cammermile, and pennyryal, and motherwort, and balm; you know, balm is very coolin', doctor" (103).

Unable to discover what ails Polly—besides the quantities of home remedies she has received— Dr. Longley expresses himself at a loss for a professional diagnosis. Hereupon Mrs. Livermore offers to fill the breach with more folk wisdom:

> "Well, now, doctor," said Mrs. Livermore, "excuse me for speakin'; but I'm a good deal older than you are, and have seen a great deal of sickness in my day, and I've been in here with Polly a number of times to-day, and sometimes this evening, and I'm satisfied, doctor, there's something the matter of her insides."
> "Undoubtedly," said the doctor, looking very grave. (105)

There is more broad sickroom comedy when, for example, the perplexed doctor says he will have to proceed in the dark—and Mrs. Gray obediently removes the candle from the room.

About one-third of the way through the story, Polly dies. The rest of the tale, which has to do with her corpse, is humor in a coarser vein than Smith usually wrote. Dr. Longley and Dr. Stubbs, another young doctor called in to consult about the case, are unable to get the family to agree to a post-mortem examination; and they resolve to steal the body from the graveyard. As Dr. Stubbs says, "I'll not only ascertain the cause of her death, but I want a subject for dissection" (111). Stubbs gets two college boys, Joe and Rufus, to do the job as a lark. Stubbs arranges to leave spades hidden for them near the graveyard; and after being well-fortified with brandy, they go to Jake Rider's livery stable to rent a horse and chaise for the night's work.

Jake, a shrewd old countryman, suspects that the boys are up to mischief. "Confound these college chaps," he says to himself; "they are always a sky-larkin' somewhere or other. . . . They are going to have a real good frolic somewhere to night. I've a plaguy good mind to jump on to one of the horses and follow, and see what sort of snuff they are up to" (115). Well-concealed by the darkness, Jake follows at a careful distance and watches the boys dig up the coffin, remove the corpse, wrap it in a sheet, and lay it in the chaise while they return to fill the grave hole. Jake creeps up, identifies the corpse, guesses that this is some scrape of the doctor's, and resolves, "I'll put a stop to this anyhow. Polly Gray was too good a sort of a gal to be chopped up like a quarter of beef" (120). He removes the body from the sheet, hides it beside the road, and conceals himself in its place. When Joe and Rufus return and discover that their corpse is alive, they leap out of the chaise and run away in fear back to the college, where they lock themselves in, convinced that either Polly has come back to life or her ghost has come to haunt them. Meanwhile, Jake reburies the body, takes the horse and chaise home, and feels well-satisfied with his night's work.

In the morning the mystified college boys visit the graveyard, where the grave appears undisturbed. They then repair to the livery stable to square accounts with Jake. He assures them that the horse and chaise came home quite safely; then, with a knowing look, he informs them that their bill is fifty dollars and adds that "dead folks tell no tales" (124). Understanding that Jake has somehow learned of their grave-robbing scheme and is really charging them for his silence, they have no recourse but to pay his exorbitant fee.

"Polly Gray and the Doctors" is one of several of the '*Way Down East* stories that contain a great deal of folklore. Smith uses New England folk medical practices and beliefs to give a rather coarse comic tone to the first half of the story, where the scene of the dying girl might have been treated sentimentally. The second part of the story fits the common folktale type: "Thieves cheated of their booty. Trickster steals the goods."[19] There is also a suggestion of the folktale motif "Return from dead to punish indignities to corpse"[20] since it expresses what the grave robbers fear has happened when their "corpse" moves. College boys are traditionally pranksters and medical students are traditionally grave robbers in folktales and anecdotes. Here young doctors get students to do the robbing for them.

There is an interesting shift in comic perspective between the first part and the second one of "Polly Gray," a duality perhaps indicative of Smith's mixed feelings about the folk. In the first section the humor is at the expense of the ignorant farm family which does not understand modern science, big words, or metaphoric language. The author seems to share the doctor's condescension toward these country folk. In the second part the roles are reversed: Jake, the unschooled livery stable man, outsmarts two doctors and two college students; and the author and the reader identify with Jake. Moreover, an obvious value judgment is implied in the contrast between the doctors' view of Polly as "a subject for dissection" and Jake's assertion that she "was too good a sort of a gal to be chopped up like a quarter of beef."

VI   *Speculators and Singing Schools*

When the *Putnam's* reviewer complained of some of the stories'
"tapering off in a disappointing manner, without any perceptible
catastrophe," he probably had in mind "The Speculator,"
"Christopher Crotchet," and "A Race for a Sweetheart." "The
Speculator" is unique among the *'Way Down East* stories in having
a villain as the main character. Colonel Kingston, a land speculator,
comes into the tranquil pastoral world of rural Maine like a serpent
into Eden; for he brings greed, ambition, domestic strife, and family ruin. He makes men who had been content with modest prosperity dream of obtaining riches. Smith had reason to suspect land
speculation, having indulged in it himself in 1837 with disastrous
results that included the loss of his interest in the *Portland Courier*.
Miss Wyman notes that he, "who had remained clear-headed and
unmoved in the midst of political broils and religious dissensions,
found himself swept into this whirl of buying and selling."[21]

In "The Speculator," Colonel Kingston, who feeds on the
villagers' newly kindled greed, maneuvers them into trading their
homes and farms for large mysterious tracts of timber land in upper
Vermont. The people of Monson Village are as easily corrupted as
the residents of Mark Twain's Hadleyburg; for even Smith's
Deacon Stone, a man noted for sober good sense, loses his grasp on
real values and risks his family's security because of his idle hope of
quick and easy riches. When a group of indignant citizens bring
charges against the speculator for swindling, he takes refuge with
the one misfit in the community, Old Johnson, a self-exiled eccentric who lives a hermit-like existence and who has some fellow feeling for another outsider. After Old Johnson has hidden the fugitive
in his cellar for two days, the speculator makes his escape; he is pursued by the townspeople, but they soon give up the chase since they
are glad to be rid of him. And so the story ends, or rather stops.

The chief interest of "The Speculator" lies in its exploration of
the folk feeling that strangers are suspect, that evil comes from outside the little world of the peasant community, and that it can be
expelled once it is identified. This simplistic vision of human affairs
assumes the Wordsworthian view that humble rural people are
naturally good. Charles A. Goodrich's *History of the United States*,
the most widely used textbook in American secondary schools
before the Civil War, and one from which Smith may have received
some of his attitudes, expresses this idea succinctly: "Those of the

country, who lead an agricultural life, preserve much of the simplicity, with something of the roughness of former days; but they enjoy all that happiness which proceeds from the exercise of the social virtues in their primitive purity."[22]

Through skillful use of dialect, surely drawn rustic character types, and effective inclusion of authentic New England folklore, Smith succeeds in the artistic creation of this ideal world in believable terms. One may consider, for example, the following brief selections which suggest the flavor of the story: " 'The deacon asked the colonel to stop to dinner, but I guess the colonel see so many sour looks about the house, that he was afraid of a storm abrewing; so he only ketched up a piece of bread and cheese, and said he must be a-goin' " (244). And a little later:

"How *did* poor Mrs. Stone feel?" asked the landlady; "I should thought she would a-died."

"She looked as if she'd turn milk sour quicker than a thunder-shower," said the teamster. (244)

"Christopher Crotchet" and "A Race for a Sweetheart" are much more cheerful vignettes of country life and folkways in the Golden Age of New England—the time of Seba Smith's own youth. The former sketch, first published in *Colman's Miscellany* for July, 1839,[23] is the more interesting because of its affectionately detailed re-creation of the institution of the singing school. It was the custom for a group of families to subscribe money enough to hire a singing master to spend several weeks in the community while boarding around at different homes. In the evenings, he would teach the young people to sing traditional songs by using the "faw, sole, law" method. Smith represents the singing school as supplying much more than musical instruction: it served as a delightful entertainment and as an ideal courting situation for the young folks. He presents the Yankee farmers and their wives as generous and affectionate toward their children and as happy to assume their share of the financial burden of the singing school so that their young people may enjoy themselves.

Just as the singing master is a figure of community interest and is much sought after by the girls in "Christopher Crotchet," the young lady schoolmarm is the center of attention from the young men of the village in "A Race for a Sweetheart." In this story another recurring motif of American mythology appears: the rich, spoiled young man loses the girl to the industrious and virtuous poor boy.

VII *Three Framework Tales*

In three of the *'Way Down East* stories that derive much of their success from Smith's use of the oral tale format—in "The Tough Yarn," "A Dutch Wedding," and "The Great Pumpkin Freshet"—a well-defined narrator is introduced in a frame story and is then permitted to tell a tale to a carefully delineated audience. "The Tough Yarn," a good story that is well-presented, combines successfully several situations and motifs of traditional American humor. The title means simply "the tall tale," "tough yarn" being one of thirty-four colloquial expressions for "incredible story" that are cited in the *American Thesaurus of Slang*.[24] The number of labels for tall tales is indicative of the central significance of such anecdotes in American vernacular humor.

In Smith's story, two members of the privileged class, Major Grant, a well-to-do Massachusetts landowner, and Dr. Snow, a prosperous local physician, meet at "a snug tavern in one of the back towns in Maine" (53) and make a wager concerning a humbler customer in the tavern, one Jack Robinson. The doctor says: " 'He's the greatest talker you ever met. I'll tell you what 'tis, Major, I'll bet the price of your reckoning here to-night, that you may ask him the most direct simple question you please, and you shan't get an answer from him under half an hour, and he shall keep talking a steady stream the whole time, too' " (55). The Yankee countryman's proverbial inability to give a straightforward answer to a simple question and his characteristic of replying to a short query with a long answer have provided the substance of numerous anecdotes in the folk tradition.[25]

Jack Robinson does not disappoint the doctor. To the major's carefully phrased question, "Is your lameness in the leg or in the foot?" (59), he replies that his father told him when he was just a boy that he should never tell where anything was unless he could first tell how it came to be there. After he has recounted several episodes from his experience, he culminates his narratives with an account of a terrible night in his eighteenth year that was spent at the mercy of "an awful great black bear, the ugliest-looking feller that ever I laid my eyes on" (68) and of some other horrible animal that he never saw but felt "the fur and hair and ears of" in the dark (73).

Robinson, one of Smith's best drawn characters, is one of a number of folk raconteurs in American literature. Like Simon Wheeler of Mark Twain's "The Celebrated Jumping Frog of Calaveras County," Robinson is garrulous and rambling; but he has closer affinities with Jim Doggett of Thomas Bangs Thorpe's "The Big Bear of Arkansas." This story was reprinted several times shortly after its 1841 publication in the *Spirit of the Times*, and it was quite possibly known to Smith from these appearances or from William Trotter Porter's anthology, *The Big Bear of Arkansas and Other Sketches* (1845).[26]

Except for Robinson's lameness, which is essential to the plot, he is presented by Smith in terms that are remarkably similar to those that Thorpe uses in introducing Doggett. Thorpe describes The Big Bear of Arkansas' entrance as follows:

The Big Bear walked into the cabin, took a chair, put his feet on the stove, and looking back over his shoulder, passed the general and familiar salute—"Strangers, how are you?" . . . There was something about the intruder that won the heart on sight. He appeared a man enjoying perfect health and contentment; his eyes were as sparkling as diamonds, and good-natured to simplicity. Then his perfect confidence in himself was irresistibly droll.[27]

One may compare with this presentation the physical appearance, expression, mannerisms, and general aplomb of Smith's storyteller:

The door opened and Mr. Jack Robinson came limping into the room, supported by a crutch, and with something of a bustling, care-for-nothing air, hobbled along toward the fire. . . . [He] was a small, brisk man, with a grey twinkling eye, and a knowing expression of countenance. As he carefully settled himself into his chair, resting his lame limb against the edge of the stove hearth, he threw his hat carelessly upon the floor, laid his crutch across his knee, and looked round with a satisfied air, that seemed to say, "Now, gentlemen, if you want to know the time of day, here's the boy that can tell ye." (55 - 56)

Leading up to their main stories, both Doggett and Robinson entertain their listeners with immodest accounts of their prowess as hunters and with tall tales about the marvels of nature in their native places. Doggett explains how in Arkansas corn shoots up overnight in a dangerous way, and Robinson tells of a neighbor who went out in the Maine woods one bad winter to gather wood and froze stiff, bolt upright. The principal anecdote with which each climaxes his narration deals with a huge, ferocious, and somewhat mysterious bear. Though both accounts contain elements of rude humor, they end on a serious note; for each storyteller expresses his awareness that he has had a memorable personal encounter with Nature in one of its terrible manifestations. Both even suggest the presence of a diabolical element: Doggett says he began to believe his bear was a devil and was hunting *him;* Robinson relates that his antagonist "looked more like Old Nick than anything I ever see before" (69). Another significant similarity between Smith's and Thorpe's stories is that in each one the readers' sympathies and identification lie with the folk raconteur, not the condescending auditors of the frame story.

Smith's effective creation of Robinson's personality and dialect, his sure touch with the folkloric elements of the anecdotes, and his skillful structuring of the frame situation make this story one of the most successful in the book. It is unfortunate that, instead of one of the insipid, didactic, undistinguished sketches like "Billy Snub" or "Peter Punctual," Smith did not include in *'Way Down East* another of his tall tales about encounters with bears, "Uncle Pete and the Bear."[28] Like "The Tough Yarn," this narrative is told by the man who claims to have had the "squabble" with "the tarnalest great overgrown bear that ever I seed in all my life." In an introductory note to the story, Smith says he heard it from an old pioneer in 1836.

Black bears were numerous in Maine during the nineteenth century—a bounty on them was offered until the 1930's—and tall stories about bears, bear hunting, and wonderful fights with bears are common in Maine folklore.[29] It is, therefore, quite possible that Smith did get the story from oral tradition. Certainly the speech of the storyteller as Smith recreates it has an air of authenticity when he recalls how the bear climbed into a canoe with him:

"As soon as he got fairly in, he looked round to me, and then he reared right up unto his hind legs and walked towards me as straight as a man. He was as tall as I was, and looked as big as a clever young ox. I stood facing of him, and while I was thinking how it was best to give battle to him, he marched right up to me, and put one paw on my right shoulder, and 'tother on my left. Thinks I, this is being a leetle too sociable for a stranger."

The incidents in Smith's two bear stories, the language, and the tone are all very close to those of the humor of the Old Southwest, particularly that of Thorpe and Crockett; and these qualities demonstrate Smith's versatility as a writer.

Another frame story, "A Dutch Wedding," is a rather slight effort; but Smith evidently liked it, since he had previously printed it in *Rover* as "Getting Over the Difficulty."[30] This sketch recounts a believable episode of backwoods life, one told by a Dutchman to a Yankee as a parable on the text that "You can often get over the difficulty, when you can't get over the river" (267). Set "about a hundred years ago . . . near where Schenectady now is, for it was a kind of wilderness place then" (270), the tale recounts the unusual circumstances of the wedding of Peter Van Horn and Betsey Van Heyden. When a flood-swollen Tomhenick River prevented the preacher from getting to the settlement, he shouted the marriage service across the river to the young couple who stood hand in hand on the other bank. When he called out that they were now man and wife, Peter threw a couple of silver dollars across the river, and the wedding party returned to Mr. Van Heyden's house for the marriage feast.

There is some interest in Smith's efforts to contrast the characters of the Yankee and the Dutchman. To the Yankee, the Dutchmen is tiresomely methodical, stubborn, and behind the times. To the Dutchman, Yankees are impatient, too competitive, and ready to try every new-fangled idea. He disdains the Yankee's loco-foco or friction matches and lights his pipe with a burning lens "out of respect to my ancestors" (268). Smith's sympathies seem to lie with the genial conservative Dutchman, who holds that "there's never anything lost by taking time to consider a matter. It is driving the steamboat too fast, and trying to get ahead of somebody else, that makes her burst her boiler" (269). As a contrast to the Dutchman, the Yankee is brash and vulgar; he exhibits unattractive aspects of the proverbial Yankee character that Smith usually does not emphasize.

One of the best pieces in *'Way Down East* is "The Pumpkin Freshet," a tale that is memorable for Smith's creation of the narrator, Aunt Patty Stow. An old pioneer woman of the Oquago Valley in New York State, she is astonished at the conveniences and comforts that she encounters on a visit to New York City. Moved by its contrast with country life, she recalls in vivid detail an episode from her childhood, sixty years before, when the little frontier community had to live for two months on pumpkins which floated down the river in a flood, "the great punkin freshet."

Like Jack Robinson of "The Tough Yarn," Aunt Patty is presented as unlettered and simple, but never as ridiculous. Their dialect is suggested as rustic but is not exaggerated; the author never condescends to them, though other characters in the story may do so. Their recollections of the excitements, terrors, and delights of their youth are full of vitality, color, and warmth. Their stories express the innocence and freshness that the narrators epitomized as youths and that they retained as a rare quality into maturity.

A sample of Aunt Patty's narrative illustrates the understated art of its style:

"And bime-by Mr. Williams, from the upper neighborhood, come riding down a horseback as hard as he could ride, to tell us to look out, for the river was coming down like a raging lion, seeking whom he may devour. He said it had run over the meadows and low grounds, and swept off the corn-fields, and washed out the potatoes, and was carrying off acres and acres of punkins on its back. The whole river, he said, was turned into a great punkin field. He advised father to move out what he could out of the house, for he thought the water would come into it, if it didn't carry the house away. So we all went to work as tight as we could spring, and Uncle Major he put to and helped us, and we carried out what things we could, and carried them back a little ways, where the ground was so high we thought the river couldn't reach 'em. And then we went home with Uncle Major Stow, and got some breakfast. Uncle Major's house was on higher ground, and we felt safe there."(328)

The archaic quality of the narrator's speech is suggested by expressions such as "Mr. Williams . . . come riding down," "a horseback," and "Uncle Major put to and helped us." The simile that likens the river to a roaring lion is in character for a Bible-reading generation for whom the scriptures provided the chief or sole source of literary allusions and exotic metaphors. All the language is close to what Wordsworth advocated as the ideal medium for poetry: the everyday speech of humble and rustic folk who have lived simple lives close to nature.

The words are all short, mostly monosyllabic. Of the 189 words in the sample passage, 148 are of one syllable, 39 of two syllables, and 3 of three syllables, and none longer. The three-syllable words *neighborhood, potatoes,* and *carrying,* are simple and homely enough. Of the two-syllable words, six are proper names; many are root-syllable plus grammatical-suffix forms (as *riding, roaring*) or

compound forms (as *horseback*). Most of the nouns are concrete
ones that name essential natural or domestic objects: *ground* (three
times), *river* (three times), *house* (three times), *fields* (twice), *water,
meadows, acres, corn, potatoes, punkins, breakfast, home, father*.
Moreover, a large percentage of verbs and verbals in the passage
contribute to the lively tone by expressing physical action: *carry*
(four times), *go* (three times), *come* (three times), *ride* (twice), *say*
(twice), *tell, look, run, sweep, get, feel, wash, think, put, help, turn,
have, work, reach, spring*. Only two of the verbs are obviously
Latinate forms: *devour*, a Biblical echo, and *advise*. There is no
vocabulary item, no grammatical form, no sentence pattern here
which fails to ring true for Aunt Patty Stow.

In the structure of the clauses and sentences, coordinate forms
predominate, giving the effect of spontaneous vernacular discourse.
And is the most frequent connective, occurring twelve times; *for* is
used conjunctively twice, and *so* once. Winston Weathers has
demonstrated that polysyndeton, as used in this passage, suggests
the past remembered, recalled by someone who is "in no hurry."
Another of Weathers' insights is that a series of more than three
items achieves an effect of "plethora, abundance, the un-
limited. . . . At times the effect is extended to that of the diversity
that is confusion. With this longer series, the writer moves from the
certainty of the two-part, from the reasonableness of three-part, to
the more complicated emotional realism of the catalogue."[31] This
generalization helps to explain the effect of excitement in the second sentence of the sample passage: "He said it had run over the
meadows and low grounds, and swept off the corn-fields, and
washed out the potatoes, and was carrying off acres and acres of
punkins on its back." Here parallelism reinforces the impact of the
series: each item consists of a verb-plus-preposition and its object,
and the series culminates in the repeated double object in the last
item—"acres and acres of punkins." Smith, who had a good ear for
American speech, could capture its nuances truly through faithful
attention to detail.

Images of plenty, of abundant food as a symbol of security and
the good life, are important in "The Pumpkin Freshet" as in
another of the *'Way Down East* sketches, "Yankee Christmas." In
both pieces, the scenes of shared food evoke a festive tone and
realize the sense of community among those who eat and drink
together. In "The Pumpkin Freshet" meager resources are lovingly
shared. Uncle Major hikes out for supplies—going forty miles to the

mill and carrying back a bushel of wheat flour on his shoulder. He tells his wife to mix it with bear grease and make shortcake, "make two milk-pans full, so as to have enough for the whole neighborhood" (333). "Bime-by," Aunt Patty remembers, "they had the table set out, and a long bench on one side, and there was two milk-pans set on the table filled up heaping full of short-cakes, and the old folks all sot down, and fell to eating, and we children stood behind them with our hands full, eating tu. And oh, them short-cakes, seems to me, I never shall forget how good they tasted the longest day I live" (337).

As a special treat, Uncle Major has brought a quarter of a pound of tea, the first the settlers have tasted in three years. "And what do you think they did for teacups?" Aunt Patty asks: "Why, they took a two quart wooden bowl, and turned off enough tea to fill it, and sot it to the table. They handed it to Major Buck first, as he was the minister, and sot to the head of the table, and he took a drink, and handed it to Uncle Major Stow, and he took a drink, and then they passed it all round the table, from one to t'other, and they all took a drink" (337 - 38).

Smith says in a note to "The Pumpkin Freshet" that the main incidents in the sketch are all historically true. As Aunt Patty recounts them, they seem believable enough; but the haunting touch of the mythic that appears in this story is suggested by the sacramental quality of the communal meal and also by the pumpkins "as yellow as gold" (325) that "kept coming along thicker and thicker, spreading away across the river, and up and down as far as we could see" (327 - 28) to sustain the little community in "the starving time" (330). They seemed a gift of the same God who cared for Noah's family in that other great flood and who sent manna to feed the children of Israel—both of which Bible stories Aunt Patty refers to in the course of her narrative (322, 326). Pumpkins were highly valued by the American settlers from earliest times, and foods prepared from pumpkins were such an important part of festive meals that certain Puritan churchmen, deploring all celebrations, derisively referred to Thanksgiving as St. Pompion's (Pumpkin's) Day.[32] Aunt Patty's suggestion that pumpkins are the manna of the New World is not unlike that expressed by Edward Johnson, a Puritan more sympathetic to pumpkins, who issued a warning in his *Wonder-Working Providence of Sion's Saviour in New England:* "Let no man make a jest at Pumkins, for with this fruit the Lord was pleased to feed his people to their good content, till Corne and Cattell were increased."[33]

VIII   *"Yankee Christmas"*

In "Yankee Christmas," the reader finds the same emphasis on
generosity and sharing as in "The Pumpkin Freshet"; but he also
finds richness in amount and in the variety of good things available.
Perhaps recalling skimpy times in his own backwoods childhood,
Smith seems to relish lists of foodstuffs, as when he has Solomon
Briggs tell his wife:

"You shall have as much Christmas as you want. There's a bushel of as
good wheat as ever was ground, I put into a bag on Saturday. . . . You've
got butter enough and lard enough in the house, and if you want any plums
or raisins, or any such sort of things, James may call at Haskall's store and
get what you want. Then Mr. Butterfield is going to kill a beef critter this
morning, and I'm going to have a quarter, so that before noon you can have
a hundred weight of beef to make your mince pies of, and if that ain't
enough, I'll send to Mr. Butterfield's for another quarter. And then there is
five heaping cart loads of large yellow punkins in the barn, and there is five
cows that give a good mess of milk; and you've got spices and ginger, and
molasses, and sugar enough in the house, so I don't see as there need be
any difficulty but what we might have punkin pies enough for all hands.
And as for the poultry, it'll be time enough to kill that to-morrow morning;
and if two turkeys aint enough, I'll kill four, besides a bushel basket full of
chickens. So now on with your birds'-egging, and make your Christmas as
fast as you please, and as much of it." (31 - 32)

"Yankee Christmas," which has little plot development, is more
like a familiar essay about the good old way of celebrating Christmas with a house full of people, ample food and drink, log fires,
many glowing candles, and general good cheer. The young folks
play games—button-button, forfeits (with much kissing), hunt the
slipper, blind man's buff, post office—and some of the old folks
cannot resist joining in the fun.

The authenticity of Smith's description of the festivities is
attested by such folklore collections as William Wells Newell's
Games and Songs of American Children and Botkin's *Treasury of
New England Folklore*. Writing in 1883, Newell said: "[In] New
England country towns of a generation since, . . . dancing, under
that name, was little practiced. . . . The amusement of young people at their gatherings was 'playing games.' These games generally
resulted in forfeits, to be redeemed by kissing, in every variety of
position and method. . . . Such were the pleasures of young men
and women from sixteen to twenty-five years of age."[34] Botkin
quotes Asa Green as writing in 1833 that the favorite party games of

young people were blindman's buff and forfeits and that "grave papa's and mama's, throwing aside their sober parental character, for the time being, assume that of frolicsome children."[35] The custom Smith describes of redeeming a forfeit by kissing through a chair back is also mentioned as traditional by Botkin.[36]

The tone of "Yankee Christmas" is pure nostalgia for an era that Smith was convinced had been a simpler and a better time. From his pleasure in recalling the festivals and pastimes of his own youth, he has provided a readable and reliable source for details about early nineteenth-century New England customs and folkways. His nostalgia is contagious.

IX "The Money-Diggers"

Another story filled with folkloric interest but one that bears no other resemblance to "Yankee Christmas" is "The Money-Diggers and Old Nick," a fully developed tale of a search for buried treasure that was first published in *Burton's* in August, 1840.[37] Leisurely in its pace, the story begins with a discussion of men's propensity to seek riches; moves to a consideration of money-diggers, searchers for buried treasure; and at last relates a particular treasure hunting expedition shortly after the Revolutionary War on Jewell's Island, off the coast of Maine.

In the plot, Bill Stanwood, a sailor who has done a good deed for a dying shipmate and who has received in return directions for finding a treasure buried by Captain Kidd, is unable to find the exact spot. Stopping at the house of a Maine farmer, Jonathan Rider, he confides his difficulty and enlists the assistance of Rider, who believes he can find the precise place to dig because of his skill with a crotched branch of witch hazel that he uses as a mineral divining rod. Asa Sampson, Rider's hired man, is skeptical but agrees to go along and help. The treasure document suggests several difficulties the searchers may encounter: the gold was buried at midnight and can be uncovered only then, and "not a word or syllable must be uttered from the time the first spade is stuck in the ground, till a handful of the money is taken out of one of the pots" (182). Most disconcerting of all, the document states that "the evil spirit of darkness is invoked to keep watch over this money" (181). Mrs. Rider is at first quite unwilling that her husband should go dig for money "right in the face and eyes of old Nick himself" (188), but she is convinced by greed to give her consent. Loaded down with a

compass, a rod pole, three shovels, a pickax, a crow bar, a supply of
hazel wands, and handkerchiefs to tie their mouths shut, the
money-diggers set out, rent a small boat at Falmouth, and row to
Jewell's Island. The homely details of their preparations and their
conversation along the way are well presented and with considerable humor.

Another note enters the story when the men arrive at the island
and seek shelter for the night at the hut of Mother Newbegin, an
old hag with some local reputation as a witch. It is said she never
sleeps but walks silently about her house all night, watching and
listening. As the treasure seekers approach her hut, they can see her
through the window, crouching by the hearth, stirring a kettle.
"The glare of the fire fell full on the old woman's face, showing her
features sharp and wrinkled, her skin brown, and her eyes black and
fiery. Her chin was leaning on one hand. . . . Her black night-cap
was on, and fastened with a piece of twine under her chin, and the
tight sleeves of her frock sat close to her long bony arms, while her
bare feet and bird-claw toes projected out in full view below the
bottom of her dress" (197 - 98). The shadow of her foot on the floor
suggests a cloven hoof. Nevertheless, the men go inside. She already
knows their errand but warns them that Old Nick takes care of his
money. When they ask about her husband, she says he has been out
fishing for three days and that, when he is ready to come home, the
wind will turn to bring him in.

After an uneasy night's sleep in the hut, the men set out at dawn;
follow the directions of the document to the general area of the
treasure; and Jonathan, who uses his mineral rod, finds, as he had
promised, the exact spot for digging. As midnight approaches, they
tie up their mouths with handkerchiefs and go to work. The night is
still, calm, and starlit when they begin; but, as the digging
proceeds, strange wild gusts of wind such as they have never experienced sweep the area, sometimes from one quarter, sometimes
another. Ominous clouds, shaped like huge animals "with a hundred eyes" (209), float overhead; and thunder begins to rumble out
of the flickering sky. Soon a heavy rain comes down, crumbling the
sides of their excavation faster than they can throw out the soil and
water. At this point "a tremendously great black dog came and
stood upon the brink, and opened his deep red jaws, and began to
bark with terrific power" (211) while springing and snapping at
them as they worked.

Despite these frightening difficulties, the money-diggers persist and at last uncover a flat stone about four feet square and six inches thick. Raising it a few inches, they probe beneath and feel four pots; but all their efforts cannot lift the stone. At this critical moment a man appears at the edge of the pit, calls off the dog, and asks, "Shall I give you a lift there?" "Yes, quick!" Asa cries (213). The moment the stranger touches the stone, it flies out of the pit, carrying the diggers with it. The stranger and the money disappear. Only four rusty holes are left, and an odor of brimstone. When the men return to Mother Newbegin's hut, she tells them that she has saved them from Old Nick: "I've kept the Bible open for you, and a candle burning before it, ever since you left the house; and I knew while the candle was shining on the Bible for you he couldn't touch you" (214).

Smith presents the story of "The Money-Diggers and Old Nick" as a traditional one:

> This island has been renowned as a place for money-digging ever since the first settlements were planted along the coast; and wild and romantic are the legends related by the old dames in the cottages of the fishermen, when some wind-bound passenger, who has left his vessel to spend the evening on shore, happens to make any inquiry about the money-diggers. But of all these wild legendary narratives, probably there is none more authentic, or supported by stronger or more undoubted testimony, than the veritable history herein recorded and preserved. (169)

The narrative as Smith presents it has all the marks of a genuine folktale. Stories of buried treasure are so popular in American culture that J. Frank Dobie has asserted that "the representative legends of America" are treasure tales; that Old World legends turn on the lure of women, New World legends on the lure of riches. [38]

In New England, stories about Captain Kidd's treasure are particularly abundant, and legends of vast riches buried by Kidd cling to Jewell's Island, though in fact Kidd never visited this part of the coast. [39] Such stories are so important a part of New England folklore that George Lunt recalls in his *Old New England Traits*, how, during holiday festivities when a lively company was gathered in the evening around the fire, his grandmother would sing the old ballad "Robert Kidd." [40] Connecticut poet John Brainard, in a note to his poem "The Money Diggers," advises those who wish to hear stories about Captain Kidd and his money to "enquire of the oldest lady you can find." [41]

Checking Smith's story against items in the *Motif-Index of Folk-Literature* reveals a number of traditional elements in "The Money-Diggers and Old Nick." The motifs may be grouped in four categories (for motif numbers see note 42): (1) Circumstances governing the time and method of the search: taboo against speaking while searching for treasure or it will disappear, between midnight and cockcrow best time for unearthing treasure, magic wand finds treasure; (2) concerning Mother Newbegin: witch's house at border of other world, witch with extraordinary feet, sleepless person of diabolical origin; (3) difficulties encountered while digging: dog guards treasure, devil in form of dog, devil as guardian of treasure, fear of threatening animals while raising treasure, storm produced by devil (associated with buried treasure), stone magically flies through air; (4) the denouement: devil exorcised with candle, devil cheated of victim by presence of Bible.[42] Many of these same folklore motifs are embodied in specifically New England legends—in tales and superstitions about buried treasure that may be found in Dorson's *Jonathan Draws the Long Bow*, in Botkin's *Treasury of New England Folklore*, and in John Greenleaf Whittier's *The Supernaturalism of New England*. These tales also reveal that the expression "money-diggers" was the traditional New England colloquialism for seekers of buried gold.[43]

These traditional, folkloristic elements account for most if not all of the similarities and influences which critics have found between Seba Smith's and other literary versions of buried treasure stories. Miss Wyman, for example, believes that Smith's Old Nick may have been suggested by Washington Irving's character Old Scratch in his story "The Devil and Tom Walker" and that the use of a divining rod to locate the treasure may have been inspired by Scott's novel *The Antiquary* in which Mr. Dousterswivel uses such a rod to locate treasure at midnight and is baffled by spirits.[44] Killis Campbell has noted a possible influence of Smith's story on Poe: "The atmospheric device of the barking of the dog in the climactic scene of *The Gold Bug* . . . was perhaps suggested to Poe by a passage in Seba Smith's *The Money Diggers*, where a similar device is employed to intensify the excitement attending the unearthing of a rich store of buried treasure. *The Money Diggers* appeared in *Burton's Magazine* in August, 1840, . . . shortly after Poe had resigned as its literary editor, and hence in all likelihood fell under his eye."[45]

Although it is not possible to show that such literary influences did not operate, no literary sources need to be sought for details such as those notices by Miss Wyman and by Campbell. Devils, divining rods, and diabolical dogs are traditionally involved in buried treasure stories. Irving, like Smith, acknowledged the traditional, oral sources of his material. "The Devil and Tom Walker" is one of three stories he included in *Tales of a Traveller* under the general title *The Money Diggers*. In the introductory remarks prefixed to the three stories, Irving not only mentions the abundance of anecdotes about Captain Kidd and about the seekers for his treasure but also tells of collecting these stories: "I sought among my favorite sources of authentic information, the oldest inhabitants, and particularly the old Dutch wives of the province." He notes that "in all the stories of these enterprises the devil played a conspicuous part."

Numerous parallels with Smith's story might be cited from Irving's money-diggers stories. In "The Adventures of Sam, the Black Fisherman," the divining rod is used; there is an injunction to silence while digging; and "snarling and growling as of a cur" is heard during a struggle between the diggers and a spirit that guards the treasure. In "The Devil and Tom Walker," Tom always keeps a Bible with him to prevent Old Scratch from carrying him off. The same kinds of parallels could be cited in Harriet Beecher Stowe's well-known Sam Lawson story "Captain Kidd's Money." Clearly, these stories indicate the use of a well-developed body of folklore by a variety of literary artists. In "The Money-Diggers and Old Nick," one of the two or three best stories in *Way Down East*, Smith is as effective in his treatment of the American treasure legend as Poe, Irving, or Mrs. Stowe.

X   *Illustrations*

The illustrations in *Way Down East* are noteworthy. The work of Nathaniel Orr, one of the country's leading wood engravers during the 1850's,[46] they are very well designed and executed; and they reflect the particular merits of the stories. Affectionate but humorous in tone, they depict with notable attention to minute and humble detail the appearance, dress, and manner of life of rustic Americans of the recent past and the settings in which that life was lived. For example, the interior of a tavern, the setting for "A Tough Yarn," shows Jack Robinson, the major, and the doctor gathered snugly around the box stove, holding tumblers of hot flip. The fat copper kettle is on, Robinson has his lame leg propped comfortably on a stick of firewood, and his hat is thrown down beside his chair. The wide, warped, rough-hewn planks of the floor are delineated; nails have been driven into the walls for hanging up odd bits of tackle; the cider barrel is drawn by a man who knew how barrels are put together; and a believable poster advertising for a stolen horse has been nailed on the cracked plaster wall. The Dickensian faces of the three men, full of character and expression, are homely and weathered without being grotesque. Every detail about them, from their scarves to their spectacles, seems just right. One imagines Seba Smith being very well satisfied with Nathaniel Orr's work.

Though the best sketches of 'Way Down East bear comparison with the work of later New England local-colorists like Harriet Beecher Stowe, Sarah Orne Jewett, and Mary Wilkins Freeman,[47] they are almost never included in anthologies. Smith's reputation as a literary artist would be enhanced by the inclusion of "The Tough Yarn," "The Money-Diggers and Old Nick," or "The Pumpkin Freshet" in anthologies of American literature.

CHAPTER 10

My Thirty Years Out of the Senate

ON April 24, 1847, Seba Smith wrote Joseph Gales and William Seaton of the Washington, D.C., *National Intelligencer* to offer to serve as that journal's New York correspondent. When they accepted next day, they directed him to mail them three letters a week; "As to topics we leave them to your judgment, improved as that is by long experience. . . . You know the conservative notions of our paper, and that knowledge will be sufficient guide on politics and philosophy. . . ."[1] Mild, learned, "soundly" conservative, the *Intelligencer* had been for half a century the country's most dependable source of political news. Established in Washington at the suggestion of Thomas Jefferson, it was, writes Frank Luther Mott, "in some respects the greatest of the long line of Washington papers."[2]

A few of Smith's reports the editors did not print; once at least they corrected him for an erroneous interpretation of the Democratic administration's policies. In the rest of his contributions, Smith was permitted to present his own inventions and ideas. By June, Smith began a satiric antiadministration series with Jack Downing as President James K. Polk's confidant. For almost a decade, from summer, 1847, to January, 1856, the Downing series continued; and, with only two omissions and with very few changes, the series was reprinted in 1859 as *My Thirty Years Out of the Senate*—a title that mocked Thomas Hart Benton's immense, two-volume work.

I *Jack Becomes President Polk's Adviser*

In this new series, Major Jack Downing appears as President James K. Polk's confidential friend and adviser. The satire is much more conventional than the 1830 - 33 creation since the content presents the personalities and the political issues of the time from a clearly Whiggish point of view and almost nothing is made of Jack's

124

pastoral origins. The style, however, remains a strong element of the art. Although at times the requirements of satire and ideology take precedence over consistency in the dialect, the language generally continues to be strongly colloquial, very easy, clear, and free. In form, the sketches are less like letters and are more dramatic because they are full of exchanges in dialogue with auctorial comments in Jack's voice. There is a marked increase in colloquial similes, common in American humor of the period; but these are not altogether appropriate in a letter, although again the letters give a strong impression of the presence of an American voice.

Jack's first meeting with Polk opens the theme—one widespread in Whig newspapers at the time—that the Mexican War is the President's personal bid for glory: " 'This war is a concern of my own getting up—for my own use; and I shall manage it jest as I please.' Says he, 'Major Downing, there's reason in all things. I don't want them Mexicans whipped too fast, especially when them upstart generals get all the glory of it' " (251). Jack quotes many passages of Polk's intimate talk that is almost as colloquial in form as his own. These expose Polk's ambition and jealousy, particularly of Generals Winfield Scott and Zachary Taylor, both aspirants to the Presidency.

II *On Manifest Destiny*

After the personality of Polk, Smith's second target is ideological—Manifest Destiny. His thematic work is "annexing," and his method is exaggeration to show the concept of Manifest Destiny as a rationalization of lust for power. As Polk's confidential representative, Jack writes from Mexico:

I hope there an't no truth in the story that was buzz'd about here in the army, a day or two ago, that Mr. Polk had an idea, when we get through annexin' down this way, of trying his hand at it over in Europe and Africa, and round there. And to prevent any quarreling beforehand about it on this side of the water, he's agoing to agree to run the Missouri Compromise line over there, and cut Europe up into Free States and Africa into Slave States. Now, I think he had better keep still about that till we get this South America business all done, and well tied up. It isn't well for a body to have too much business on his hands at once (273).

The satire of imperial ambition is clear. Jack is also less humble with Polk than he was with Jackson; he is more obviously the cracker-barrel philosopher of "common sense" advice.

In addition to Jack's direct statement, Smith also attacks the fanaticism and danger of Manifest Destiny in a dream-allegory:

I dreamt t'other night that we had got through annexin' all North and South America; and then I thought our whole country was turned into a monstrous great ship of war, and Cape Horn was the bowsprit, and Mr. Polk the captain. And the captain was walking the deck with his mouth shet, and everybody was looking at him and wondering what he was goin' to do next. At last he sung out, "Put her about; we'll sail across now and take Europe, and Asha, and Africa in tow—don't stop for bird's-egging round among the West India Islands; we can pick them up as we come back along—crowd all sail now and let her have it."(281)

The ship sails faster; the many nationalities that make up the crew cannot work well together in the storm and start mutinies; she finally runs aground; and ship and crew are lost. Pride and ambition destroy the ship of state.

The concept of Manifest Destiny included two ideas: the moral regeneration of the world by force of example and the extension of authority over the Western hemisphere and beyond. As Russel B. Nye argues in *This Almost Chosen People,* "The search by Americans for a precise definition of their national purpose, and their absolute conviction that they have such a purpose, provide one of the most powerful threads in the development of an American ideology."[3] This vision of Manifest Destiny, shaped by countless politicians, leading citizens, and newspaper editors, achieved mythic magnitude. The guiding image drew together the loose conglomeration of diversified cultures and isolated communities that comprised the early republic. Masses of average men responded with religious passion. Manifest Destiny gave an answer to man's eternal need for a sense of large community and national identity, and his pride expanded because of his sense of participation in a divine purpose. Seba Smith and conservatives like him saw danger to the individual character, to the American nation, and to the peoples of the world in establishing democracy as a popular religion and Manifest Destiny as a moral imperative. As a result, he identified pride, self-righteousness, and aggression as the destructive elements in the myth of Manifest Destiny.

In Smith's series about the Mexican War, he repeats his general uneasiness over war itself. Several passages present visions of dead or wounded soldiers, both Mexican and American. Smith humanizes the Mexican soldier or farmer to present him as victim in his own

land. Jack hard-heartedly advises Polk to send settlers so that, "as
fast as we killed a Mexican, or drove him off from his farm, we
could put an American right on to it" (284). The cruel inhumanity
of Jack's modest proposal has great satiric vigor.

Smith expresses both the danger of the adventure in Mexico and
the essential evil of war in a story that Jack tells of Bill Johnson.
Polk is mistaken, Jack writes, in his conviction that peace can be
conquered:

> It's a good deal as 'twas with Bill Johnson, when he and I was boys, and he
> undertook to conquer a hornet's nest, expectin' to get lots of honey. He
> took a club, and marched bravely up to it, and hit it an awful dig, and
> knocked it into a thousand flinders.
> "There, blast ye," says Bill, "I guess you're done tu now," as he begun to
> look around for the honey. But he soon found 'twasn't conquered—'twas
> only scattered. And presently they begun to fly at him, and sting him on all
> sides. . . . At last Bill found he should soon be done tu, himself, if he
> stayed there, so he cut and run.
> "Hullo," says I, "Bill, where's your honey?"
> "Darn it all," says he, "if I hain't got no honey, I knocked their house to
> pieces; I've got that to comfort me." (280)

Through this tale of disappointed expectation, Smith presents both
the danger of the American adventure in Mexico and the irrational
evil present in the aggression. The tale presses the reader to con-
front not only greed, which is comprehensible, but revenge and joy
in destruction, which are the darkest human motives. The blunt
meaning, however, is softened in the tradition that the tale is "only
a funny story." The vehicle, Bill Johnson, is a character type of less
than average humanity. The symbolism of the parable transforms
the Mexican nation into a hornets' nest, a far from sentimental image. However made palatable by the forms of humor, the meaning
of Bill Johnson's "comfort" opens to contemplation the human
need to torture and destroy.

III   *On Slavery*

Markedly subordinated in Smith's satire is any evaluation of the
"peculiar institution" of slavery. As far as his writing reveals,
slavery presented itself to Seba Smith not as a human or ethical
problem but as a political one. His treatment of slavery in his 1849
vision of the consequences of sectionalism is unenlightening. To instruct the Downingville Democrats, Uncle Joshua recounts an ex-

emplary family history of the quarrels and eventual reconciliation of
two brothers. The allegory represents the United States as a produc-
tive farm, the North-South division as a fence, Mexico as the family
of Silverbuckles, California as a gold-apple orchard, and the slaves
of the Southern branch of the family as thistles. The allegory
prophesies secession, impoverishment for both families, and
military defeats to the South from Mexico and to the North from a
combination of Mexico, South American states, and Great Britain.
After the loss of Texas and California, the families reunite for common security.

In effect, the allegory is feeble: the family quarrel is a stock image for factionalism, and the two branches of the family are not distinguished from each other. The images of Silverbuckles for Mexico, of Goldthreads for South American nations, and of Boheas for
the English are not enlightening symbols; and to use the image of
the slaves as thistles is ugly and dehumanizing. To be black in the
United States in the 1840's and 1850's, as Frederick Douglass' books
testify, was a maddening experience; but no evidence exists in
Smith's work that his moral imagination made any effort to conceive blacks as members of humanity. The point he really makes in
the allegory is that quarrels are politically unprofitable. Still, for all
its weakness as comic art, this work clings to the Whigs' most
positive purpose: the preservation of the Union.

Smith's uneasiness over the breakup of the Democratic and Whig
parties is a recurrent theme in the decade following the Mexican
War. Stylistically, he expresses his vision of political chaos through
frequent use of long lists that achieve a comic effect through juxtaposition of names, unexpected contrasts, and sheer length:

There would be the Union Whigs, and the Abolition Whigs, and the Union
Democrats, and the Abolition Democrats, and the Silver Gray Whigs, and
the Wooly-head Whigs, and the Hunker Democrats, and the Barn-burner
Democrats, and the Seward party, and the Union Safety Committee party,
and the old Abolition party, and the regular Free-sile party, and the regular
Vote-Yourself-a-Farm party, and the old Secession party, and the Co-
operation Secessionists, and the Out-and-out unqualified Go-alone
Secessionists, all in the field, and every one fightin' on their own hook.
(345)

The extravagance of polysyndeton, the excessive parallelism, and
the folksy party names are comic. As the series continues, the names
increase in length, achieving a disordered, mad effect.[4] Since Smith

feared the country could not deal with its problems if such political splintering and decay continued, Uncle Joshua urges a return to two parties; but he concludes that "how it's to be done, puzzles me and worries me a good deal" (345). Nonetheless, Jack maintains, with his brainless faith in "common sense," that a way out of every difficulty exists.

IV *Presidential Politics in 1852*

For the Presidential campaign of 1852, Smith invented some vigorous anti-Democratic political comedy. Ideologically, his satire rests on the repeated charge that the Democrats lack principles and cling blindly to personalities and to the past. His technique is to use Downingville as the political Democratic microcosm and, through a series of burlesque convention reports and burlesque minutes, to expose the hidden party motives. These motivations include selfishness, hunger for office, attempts to conceal lack of principle, and a tendency to cling to legalisms and tradition to hide the lack of moral purpose and direction.

After Franklin Pierce was nominated at the Baltimore Democratic National Convention in June, 1852, Smith managed a series of witty strokes on the theme of Pierce as a leader without a past, without principles, and without purpose—in short, as a non-person. Jack reports to the editors of the *Intelligencer* that Uncle Joshua fears that electing Pierce will be difficult. After Jack returns from the convention, Uncle Joshua asks him, "Major, who is *Gineral Pierce?* It ain't a *fictitious* name, is it?" (384). Unintentionally, Jack reveals that he, too, has had doubts about Pierce's reality. To assure himself of Pierce's existence, on his way back from Baltimore, Jack had gone through New Hampshire to ask in Concord about the nominee. "The neighbors there all knew him perfectly well, and showed me the house he lives in. He wasn't at home, or I should a seen him myself" (384 - 85). When Uncle Joshua, fearing a hoax, persists with "Well, now, Major, are you sure there is such a person . . . ?," Smith delivers his wittiest stroke: "Yes," says Jack, "Uncle, I'm as sure of it as I am that there is such a person as Uncle Joshua Downing" (384).

Although somewhat more real as a person than Uncle Joshua Downing, Franklin Pierce was a rather unlikely New Hampshireman. His administration was either generally uninspired or expansionist and pro-Southern. Hawthorne's campaign biography of his old Bowdoin friend, who believed that slavery was entitled to

protection under the Constitution, cost him many friends; and
Sophia Peabody Hawthorne felt called upon to mount a vigorous
offensive of explanations to the Peabody family and to their liberal
connections.[5]

Before 1852 was ended, Jack reported with joy what Seba Smith
felt with sorrow—that "Gineral Pierce has killed the Whig party"
(399). When Pierce's election launched Jack on his last adventure as
Presidential adviser, the theme of his final letters is America's in-
terference in the affairs of other nations. Since Smith is generally
anti-Young America, anti-expansionist, and anti-imperialist, he has
Jack quote enthusiastically General Caleb Cushing's summer, 1853,
oratorical vision of America as the modern Rome that is destined to
obey a law of expansion: "How was it with old Rome? She conquered. She went on annexin' according to the law of her existence,
and so long as she proceeded in the application of that law of her
existence, no earthly power could withstand her progress. I say that
was the destiny of ancient Rome, and it is the destiny of modern
Rome. . . . I say . . . for us a Divine voice has said, March, march,
march . . ." (412). God, the laws of nature, and the dignity of
history are all invoked to support American conquests of other
nations.

However, it is not merely the ambition and fanaticism of
politicians that Smith satirized; in the same passage he ridicules
that marked bellicosity of rural America, where such spread-eagle
oratory had its strongest following. Down in Maine, writes Jack,
Cushing's speech "came over Cousin Sargent Joel like a streak of
lightning"; he scoured up his old firelock and spent days tramping
about the house and barn, chanting "march, march, march" (412).
Here Smith scores infantile aggression that is awaiting its object.
The quick response of country folk in these final letters becomes less
a matter of courage or moral purpose than a primitive susceptibility
to the excitement of war—one reflected by Joel's incantatory chanting and marching.

As Pierce's Minister-General, Jack tours Europe. Whenever he
wishes to get his own way, he shows his commission. "The fact is,"
Jack writes Pierce, "Europe's afraid of us. I think we are fast getting
the upper hand. There ain't another nation in all creation, without
'tis Russia, that hardly dares to say her soul's her own, for fear we
shall be down upon her, and take her soul away from her" (415).
Although Jack's diction creates a mixed tone, Smith's intent is clear:

Jack's provincial intolerance, when combined with power, creates a threat to all other cultures.

Jack performs his international aggressions in a drab surtout and a broad-brimmed hat—dress that is emblematic of Republican simplicity. By these symbols Smith satirizes the disjunction between the ideals of modesty, tolerance, and honesty, and the national practices of aggression against and intolerance of other cultures. Humbly dressed according, in fact, to administration regulations, Jack plots imperial ambitions. When European nations go to war, Jack advises Pierce in a sample of "common sense," "It'll be jest the time for us to strike, and go to annexin', and carry out our manifest destiny in a handsome manner" (417). Jack approves of Commodore Matthew C. Perry's opening "the oyster-shell of Japan" (417), and he advises that China and the Pacific islands be annexed on the way home.

V *Jack Supports the Ostend Manifesto*

As an expression of Democratic aggressiveness, the Ostend Manifesto received Smith's attention in March, 1855. This document—prepared as a confidential diplomatic report by Pierre Soulé, John Y. Mason, and James Buchanan, the United States ministers to Spain, France, and Great Britain—declared, in effect, that Cuba was indispensable to the security of slavery. In Smith's letter, which plays comically with the aggressive element of the Manifesto, he first shows Jack's excitement over conquering Cuba. Second, he creates a fictional dialogue between Soulé and a spokesman for the Queen of Spain that rehearses American grievances in such a way as to show them to be trivial and contrived: Soulé's tone is insulting and provocative.

Smith's third strategy is to quote portions of the Manifesto, which had just been published. The incredible language of the document, invoking "every law, human and divine" in "wresting Cuba from Spain," was itself absurd. As for the Manifesto declaration that "The Union can never enjoy repose, nor possess reliable security as long as Cuba is not embraced within its boundaries," Smith repeats it thematically three times, because such repetition emphasized the element of physical absurdity in the language and in the paranoid logic that, not until the rest of the world was "embraced" within the boundaries of the United States could such passion for security be consummated and achieve "repose." Seba Smith never directly perceives the vague aura of sexuality in decent America's aggressions, but his comic sense often was bemused by its imperialistic diction.

VI *Jack as Filibusterer*

Filibustering in Cuba provides the adventures for Jack's final two letters. He hears that the United States has a secret agent in Cuba contacting disaffected men, ones whom Jack identifies as "leading patriots" (441). Curious to learn the agent's identity, Jack is delighted to discover it is Jefferson Davis, who was, in fact, then Pierce's Secretary of War. "If Jeff. Davis is in Cuba," writes Jack, "the thing is done, and no mistake about it" (443). Jack soon learns that the Cuban uprising has failed, that the United States has made no open move to support it, that United States attorneys are suddenly and unexpectedly enforcing the neutrality act, and that many Cuban "patriots" have been executed on the island. The underhanded intervention has brought death to some faraway people, but Jack, alive and unscathed, is ever optimistic about the morality of liberating oppressed people: "it was all an accident, and nobody to blame" (446). Smith's moral distaste for the self-serving quality of such "common sense" assessments is clear.

Besides interventionism, Smith satirizes the practice of justifying violence in terms of ideology. When Jack fears that the navy might not bombard Havana, he invokes what was felt to be at the time "idealistic" rhetoric to express his disappointment: "Is liberty going to be crushed out . . . is there any chance yet for them poor fellers that have been trying so long and so hard to get their freedom?" (441). Jack's words are cant. In his dialect, dress, actions, and ideas, he has no measure but the practice of his own community. By freedom Jack means for the Cubans to be like himself. The more he uses the word *freedom*, the quicker he is to bombard Moro Castle or to "whip them beastly Mormons that's got so many wives" (457).

As Jack moves from the national to the international scene, his provincial standards appear as principally negative ones and lead him usually to disapproval of others. He carries to London and Paris those strong, mysterious ties of psychic identification with his little community which absolutely prevent him from knowing or imagining selves unlike himself. From politicians and from the press Jack learns to rationalize his own impulses in terms of national "ideals."

Returned to Washington, Jack is assured by Pierce that his administration's support of the neutrality laws is mere political necessity. Privately, he wants Cuba as much as Jack does. To assure renomination at the upcoming convention, Pierce needs to call attention to himself as president; and his method is to provoke trouble with Denmark, England, or Nicaragua. However, starting a conflict is complicated; he needs something more. "The greatest difficulty now," Pierce tells Jack, "is with this confounded stiff-necked, stupid Congress" (454). The House of Representatives is deadlocked over choosing a speaker, and Pierce wants the Congress to be so organized that it can take part of the responsibility for whatever war he manages to promote.

Jack lobbies among the members but cannot change any votes. When he reports his failure, Pierce, in a manner which reminds Jack of Old Hickory, declares that by hook or crook the House must have a Speaker. Jack sees but one last chance, and "that is, for me to go and bring the Two Pollies [his ship] round here, and bring her guns to bear on the Capitol. Then send in word, and give them one hour to organize. If they don't do it, then batter down the house about their ears, or march in the Downingville melitia and drive 'em out, as old Cromwell did the Rump Parliament" (456). Before Pierce can consent to fire on congressmen, he spends a moment in deep study. Then, with a proverb to help him think—"a desperate disease sometimes needs a desperate remedy"—Pierce tells Jack, in Davy Crockett's words, that, if he thinks he is right, he is to go ahead.

Thus *My Thirty Years Out of the Senate* ends on the note which opened Jack's political adventures in 1830: he watches a legislative body that is unable to organize itself. But now the old Major has been formed by the Jacksonian revolution. He is deeply implicated in Pierce's efforts to shape events and to use Congress to serve his private ambitions. Smith images the doughface Pierce as without intelligence or principle, as clinging to the presidency by any means, but, paradoxically, as feeble rather than vigorous. Congress seems equally feeble. Evocation of Cromwell's England is an ominous extravagance. But the irresponsible Jack feels only joy for the coming storm.

The last letters are more significant as political satire than as portraits of Yankee characters and ways. Jack, who becomes increasingly one-dimensional, is a persona who satirizes the Democratic administration for the prestigious *National Intelligencer*. Each of the letters includes at least one issue of the time. The number of historical personalities engaged for evaluation or for ridicule is large. Many such characters appear dramatically through fictions of speech and action; they are presented as abstractions of vices rather than as whole human beings. The Mexico and Europe that Jack visits are not created as concrete places, and Downingville itself appears only rarely and is then limited as symbol or in allegory. However, the satire remains vigorous because the issues that Smith engages are generally significant and because his points are serious and weighty ones that are addressed by an intelligent and integrated conservative.

VII *Jack's Last Adventure*

When *My Thirty Years Out of the Senate* appeared in 1859, it included most of the 1834 *Life and Writings*, one revised sketch from *John Smith's Letters*, and omitted *May-Day in New York*; consequently, it represents Smith's final presentation of the life and adventures of Major Jack Downing. Smith revised the many stylistic peculiarities of the first volumes. He added quotation marks throughout, but somewhat inconsistently; he regularized some spellings; and he changed "would n't" to "wouldn't" to the general improvement of the text. The volume contained sixty-four original wood engravings, designed mostly by Justin H. Howard and executed by Nathaniel Orr, John William Orr, James H. Richardson, and several others. Finally, clear, well-spaced print adds to an attractive volume.

The book's broadest theme is an amiable presentation of the common man and a deflation of the myth of his capacities to direct the national destiny. His commonness, which, in its place, charmed Smith (and anywhere charmed many of his readers), is the very characteristic which disables him for leadership. Ingenuously, without any sense of his vanity, this common man takes himself as he finds himself; and he affirms as models for the world his own opinions, preferences, and tastes.[6] The concept of the disinterested thinker does not exist for him; the question of quality does not occur to him. Mormons are beastly to him; he scorns hoeing potatoes; he seeks only his own ease; he is delighted with himself; and he does not suspect that thought, knowledge, or effort are necessary to make the political system work. That the civilization which supports him is the product of unusual minds and that its maintenance requires unusual efforts are concepts that do not occur to Jack. To him, the political system, like nature, is given. His is "the absurd state of mind" of the masses as Ortega y Gasset sees it: "they are only concerned with their own well-being, and at the same time they remain alien to the cause of that well-being."[7] To the old conservative, Seba Smith, this absurdity is the central comic element in Jack's being.

However, neither Smith's attitudes nor Jack's absurdities are universally apparent today. Jacksonianism has triumphed. Jack's easy self-confidence, his pursuit of success, his love of adventure and action, his belief in common sense and in the consequent simplistic formulations and solutions are established in the myth of the common man.

While the politics of the letters devoted to Polk and Pierce are of limited interest, the details of humor remain sharp to the end. The total theme is filled out, like the design of a Dutch painting, with subtle plays on common linguistic and thought patterns: "Although I've got through 'My Thirty Years Out of the Senate' " writes Jack in his postscript, "I aint agoing to sit down and do nothin'—I aint one of that nater; and as it's pretty likely I shall be out of the Senate some time longer if I live, I shall keep sturrin' round, writin' for the good of the country, or fightin' for the good of the country, as long as I can hold out" (547). The satire on activism, the play on cant, the play on the sound of words, the play on rhetorical structure, and the play on the inversion of logic of "if I live"—all are rich in comicalities of form and meaning. The meaning aside, these esthetic features give pleasure to the reader.

VIII *Declining Years*

Smith was sixty-seven years old when *My Thirty Years Out of the Senate* was published. Although he lived nearly another decade, this volume virtually marked the end of his literary production. During 1859 he and Elizabeth edited *The Great Republic* and probably wrote some of this publication's historical sketches, stories, and plays; but the journal, hopefully advertised as "tolerant, wide awake, discreet, conscientious, and pure," did not last beyond the first year.[8] By 1866 a literary gossip column was noting that Smith had not written anything for several years; but Elizabeth, who was to survive him for twenty-five active years, was at work on her autobiography and on a play about Oliver Cromwell.[9]

Suffering from increasing deafness, illness, and partial paralysis,[10]

Smith lived his last years in seclusion at Patchogue, Long Island, where, as Elizabeth wrote to a friend, his only enjoyment was "reading his paper, and his game of chess with me in the evening."[11] On July 28, 1868, he died. Following her husband's desires, Elizabeth commended him to the world on his gravestone, not as humorist, but as "Poet and Scholar."

CHAPTER 11

The Critical Reception

TODAY, many students of American literature accept Smith's *The Life and Writings of Major Jack Downing* and, less often, his *'Way Down East* as minor but significant contributions to the national letters. Jack Downing, in his various Yankee metamorphoses, has entered the national pantheon as one of the grand types of the American character; for ignorant or wise, he is the active, hopeful common man. But Seba Smith himself did not consider the *Life and Writings* to be a significant work of art nor Jack to be a respectable persona. In an 1852 letter to Bowdoin College, he declined an invitation to appear at his alma mater's commencement with remarks in the character of Jack. "I am afraid 'Major Downing' would be somewhat out of place in a commencement exercise," he explained, not flattered.[1]

Two years later, replying to a request for a list of his publications, he wrote: "I have published but one volume that I think of much account, and that is the 'New Elements of Geometry.' Most of my other writings consist of fugitive articles in prose and verse, which have appeared in periodicals. . . . The Downing letters were remarkable for their extensive circulation and very great popularity, which I conceive arose more from peculiar circumstances than from their intrinsic merit."[2] Smith's sense of propriety and his conservative perspective undervalue his comic work. What he saw as the "peculiar circumstances" of Jacksonian America and of Jack's response posed in reality a perennial set of questions about democracy.

I *First Responses*

The respectable journals of the early republic did not notice the Jack Downing letters. By June, 1845, however, the newly established *American Review* engaged itself in the literary wars of the decade by printing an attack on pleas for a native American literature. Jack Downing appeared in the essay as an example of the absurd and ignoble form that nativist literature might take:

Is there an American school of writers? None, certainly, unless they who degrade and vulgarize the tongue and the taste of the country by performances, the whole merit of which consists in their adoption of particular local slang (such as was employed in Major Downing's Letters, or in the lucubrations of Sam Slick) are the models of a new and noble literature that is to be for us. When these things shall found for us a *learning*, The Ethiopian Minstrels will create for us a Music, and the disciples of Jim Crow a Theater of our own.

While Whig in politics and therefore potentially sympathetic to Smith's work, the *Review* was devoted to the Victorian ideal of "seriousness," distrusted the new, and disapproved of the vernacular style.

Significantly, it was a newspaper, the New York *Evening Gazette*, which undertook to defend Smith by drawing parallels between the Downing letters and Robert Burns's work, by calling attention to European interest in the music of Negro minstrels, and specifically by crediting Smith with a contribution to American literature's "intellectual independence." Smith quoted this exchange in the Postscript to *May-Day in New-York* (1845). This volume also includes, as has been noted, a prefatory history of "Downing literature" that reprints several newspaper comments about the letters; and thereby indicates that the popular journals were the first to perceive the newness, ease, flexibility and consequent power of Smith's language and to recognize that his work constituted a minor stylistic revolution.

The most noteworthy response to the letters, in fact, was their popular success. Mary Alice Wyman's survey indicated that, before the book of 1833 was published, many of Jack's letters were reprinted and imitated in over thirty newspapers between 1830 and 1833. Her statistics reveal but a fraction of the actual reprint history of the letters.[3] Seba Smith himself wrote that *The Life and Writings* had "eight or nine" editions through Lilly, Wait, and Company.[4] In *Golden Multitudes*, Frank Luther Mott lists *The Life and Writings* as a runner-up to the best seller for 1833. *May-Day in New-York* had two editions in 1845. Smith's final collection of the letters, *My Thirty Years Out of the Senate*, had enthusiastic responses from newspapers throughout the United States.[5]

Before 1865, C. A. Davis' imitations had ten editions in New York and two in London; and at least four other spurious and pirated editions had appeared in the United States and England.[6] Poor Smith's troubles with decent editions are not yet over. In 1970, Gregg Press reprinted as Seba Smith's work *Select Letters of Major Jack Downing*, an 1834 Philadelphia pirated edition with a grotesque "Prefase" not by Smith and lacking his "My Life."

Theater productions also attested to Jack Downing's popularity. During 1834 - 35 several plays on the New York stage presented Jack and his Downingville kin. James Hackett presented *Major Jack Downing* at the Park Theater, in the spring, 1834. Next spring, at the same theater, George H. Hill played Jack in *The Lion of the East*.[7] The title invites comparison between Jack and Nimrod Wildfire, the tall-talking Southwestern frontiersman of James K. Paulding's *The Lion of the West*. Both characters are projects in the search for the distinctive American character. Jack as a stage figure appeared as recently as the mid-1960's when Willian Mooney presented "*Major Jack Downing Goes to Portland*, by Seba Smith" at the Players Theatre on New York's off-Broadway circuit.[8]

By 1859, the journalists' old affection for Jack sometimes grew extravagant. The *New Yorker* announced on April 9 that "No richer and racier volume of Yankee humor has ever been presented to the American public." The Providence, Rhode Island, *Daily Post* noted "These papers have had a wide circulation and a great popularity, not only on account of the genial humor and infinite drollery which pervades them, but also because underneath this peculiarity is many a quaint truth asserted, and many a political moral pointed out." The Saugerties *Telegraph* of April 4 printed the assessment that "This work may justly be classed as the 'Don Quixote' of American Literature." The Glen's Falls, New York, *Messenger* for April 15 headlined its review "Not for a day, But for All Time." The quality of the humor was characterized as rich, racy, pungent, quaint, sly, "written in the tone and genuine spirit of Yankeedom, and clothed in the real vernacular of the land."[9]

In the popular imagination, Jack came to represent the American people and was so portrayed in political cartoons of the 1830's and 1840's. Traditionally drawn in top hat, tailed coat, and striped trousers, the Jack Downing of the cartoonists influenced the evolution of the familiar symbolic figure of Uncle Sam.[10]

Poe, in his "Chapter on Autobiography" in *Graham's Magazine*, December, 1841, played with the problem of who really wrote the

Downing letters. Taking but little pleasure in the homely, Poe never addressed himself to the quality of the style or of meaning in the work. In the *Dial*, 1843, Emerson, with characteristic perception of style, praised in Davy Crockett and in Jack Downing a "new and stronger tone."[11]

The most influential anthologists of the first half of the nineteenth century, Rufus W. Griswold and the Duyckinck brothers, assign Smith a minor status, mentioning him but not including his work. In *The Prose Writers of America* (1847), Griswold mentions only Smith's Downing letters, saying that through them runs "a very genuine humor of a certain sort." Somewhat more specifically, George and Evert Duyckinck write in the monumental *Cyclopaedia of American Literature* (1855) that the letters are "among the most successful adaptations of the Yankee dialect to the purposes of humorous writing." Both anthologies present Smith's significant contribution as being in the use of language and in the comic mode.

In England, the critical establishment was earlier and fuller in its treatment of American humor. John Murray, in 1835, commissioned an article "Major Downing's letters," for the *Quarterly Review*. When the *Westminster Review* for December, 1838, assessed seven volumes of American humor, the writer observed that "these books show that American literature has ceased to be exclusively imitative." Southwestern rather than New England humor most attracted the essayist. Thomas Chandler Haliburton's three-volume *Traits of American Humor* (1852) reprinted "My First Visit to Portland." For January, 1852, the *Westminster Review* published an ambitious "Retrospective Survey of American Literature" which included Seba Smith among the contributors to an "original and for the most part national comedy." Generally, English reviewers were most impressed with the tall tale and with the extravagance of Southwestern American humor, but they found the New England contribution both distinctive and original. Throughout the rest of the nineteenth century, Smith's Jack Downing volume was reprinted in English editions, represented in English anthologies, and praised by English critics.[12]

II *Some Writers Read Smith*

From the time of Smith's death until World War I, he received virtually no attention from academic critics or from the editors of the influential American magazines. James S. Cox, in *Why We*

Laugh (1880), gives him only the most casual references; and Edmund Clarence Stedman's eleven-volume *Library of American Literature* (1889 - 91) includes only three selections from the Downing letters.

Several successful American humorists offered the implied praise of imitation. Willian Tappan Thompson's Major Jones letters are echoic in form and content; Artemus Ward acknowledged his indebtedness to Smith;[13] Mark Twain, an impressive student of the artists in American humor, listed Seba Smith in his notebooks (1879 - 1882) as he began plans for his *Library of Humor*.[14] When the anthology finally appeared in 1888 after extensive work on it by William Dean Howells, it included one selection from the opening essay, "My Life," and the spurious "Uncle Joshua in Boston," which Smith had included in his own 1833 and subsequent editions. Both episodes present the Yankee as trickster.

III   *Reinterpretations*

After 1918, as after the Revolution, Americans again asked themselves, with the new self-consciousness of world power, who they were. The change in international status stimulated an extensive reevaluation of American literature; the establishment of Melville's reputation exemplifies this reconsideration. During this critical ferment, American humor profited from the new quest for national identity and from the new perspectives furnished in time by esthetics, psychology, history, folklore studies, and philosophy. The four-volume *Cambridge History of American Literature* (1917 - 21)—edited by William P. Trent, John Erskine, Stuart P. Sherman, and Carl Van Doren—dealt seriously with the early humorists:

First in point of time among the new humorists came Seba Smith (1792 - 1868), whose *Letters of Major Jack Downing* appeared in 1830. Almost immediately after his graduation from Bowdoin College in 1818, Smith began to contribute a series of political articles in the New England dialect to the papers of Portland, Maine. These illustrated fairly well the peculiarities of New England speech and manners, and doubtless had a great influence in encouraging similar sketches in other parts of the country. . . . He was the first in America . . . to create a homely character and through him to make shrewd comments on politics and life. (II, 151)

Within a few years, students at Columbia University were doing graduate work in American humor under the direction particularly of Carl Van Doren and William Peterfield Trent.

V. L. O. Chittick's seven hundred-page *Thomas Chandler Haliburton* (1924) illustrated what enlightened and indefatigable scholarship could do with a minor humorist. Chittick credited Seba Smith with "the definite beginning of the 'down east' tradition in American humor" (367). The next year, Jennette Tandy offered in *Crackerbox Philosophers in American Humor and Satire* the first extended scholarly treatment of the homely, unlettered philosopher in American literature. Her central theme grasped one of the major impulses in this humor. Although she does not discuss the nature of folk humor (for which there was no theoretical material at the time), she glimpsed the traditional in Smith's work in her assertion that a "long succession of Yankee yarns precedes the appearance of Jack Downing" (x).

After a chapter about backgrounds of the comic Yankee, she devotes to Jack six pages of excellent analysis: "The Major is on the whole his own best critic of political practices. His running comments in which he sustains the character of an ignorant, none too scrupulous hanger-on, while they lack wit, are the shrewdest irony, and far surpass his simple burlesques and clumsy parables" (28). Miss Tandy undervalues burlesques, which Smith perceived as a common form in folk humor. He saw that the folk cultivate humor and that the resulting culture of humor provides them with both forms and meanings to judge the standard culture. But this element in Smith's work, which provides it with some of its deepest resonance, was virtually impossible to discuss in the 1920's. One consequence of failure to perceive the contrastive world of folk humor is that Miss Tandy concludes about Charles Augustus Davis' letters that the "imitator excels and overshadows his original."[15]

Also from the group of scholars at Columbia University came the only book-length study devoted to the Smiths: Mary Alice Wyman's *Two American Pioneers: Seba Smith and Elizabeth Oakes Smith*. Factual rather than critical, Miss Wyman's book is indispensable to any student of these two writers. Through a granddaughter of the two writers, Miss Wyman had access to a large collection of family papers—now mostly at the University of Virginia and in the New York Public Library. These she examined carefully, identified minor figures, and studied regional and local histories as well as standard works in order to produce a volume packed with detailed information. She has given some attention to almost all the writing that both Seba and Elizabeth produced—a staggering task.

Constance Rourke, in her search for an American esthetic tradition, examined folk culture for the roots of native art. Consequently, she read Seba Smith with great sympathy and perception. Her *American Humor: A Study of the National Character* (1931) places Smith among the significant contributors to the national pantheon of character types. Except for attributing to Smith the spurious Uncle Joshua episode (the power of the Yankee pictured as a cheat draws even the greatest planets out of orbit), she shows a strong command of Smith's meaning and style. Jack she sees as slipping outside local legend to become part of the national myth: "lucid and large," she writes, "he belongs with the Yankee of the fables." Like Jennette Tandy, she sees Jack as "the Yankee emerged in a new role, as oracle."[16] In this present study, we regard Smith's spokesman in his satiric dimension as a creature of foolishness and incapacities: in line with ancient comic figures, Jack triumphs by vital energy rather than by oracular powers or common sense. To Rourke, Jack's immense popularity is ironic: the humble character would be "expected to exalt rather than to puncture the workings of democracy."

As a student of Smith's technique, Miss Rourke considered understatement to be his essential quality. Understatement, she says, is representative of Yankee humor generally, which is always distinguishable from the violent and extravagant humor of the Old Southwest: "The low key of the Yankee was maintained against the rhapsody of the backwoodsman. Yankee humor was gradual in its approaches, pervasive rather than explicit in its quality, subtle in its range.[17] As satire, she sees Smith's work as "delicately edged."

Later, in "A Note on Folklore," Miss Rourke called for a more effective criticism of style and, most importantly, presented the definitive evaluation of Smith's achievement:

Our own traditions in the matter of folk-language are not brought into useful play. A hundred years ago, Seba Smith created an effect of Yankee speech without making its oddities obtrusive, in a medium that is all but transparent, and, if one cares to notice it, very beautiful, revealing without effort the slow abundant satire. A small number of now forgotten writers accomplished something of the same effect at about the same time; indeed within that formative period many of the characteristic rhythms and colors of American speech became clear. But these early conquests were nearly obliterated by Lowell's attempt at a crackling realism in *The Biglow Papers,* and many another dark abyss in the use of the native language yawned afterward. Occasionally the more sensitive uses have been maintained; but in the intervening years these have generally been forgotten, and it is probably safe to say that many writers of the present day who use folk materials, even within the New England tradition, do not know the work of the quiet journalist of Maine. In college courses *The Biglow Papers* are likely to have a place when Seba Smith's *Downing Papers* [sic]—in all ways true originals, and of far greater social importance—are neglected.[18]

Her sense of Smith's control, of his sure touch with the colloquial, and her appreciation of the plenitude of meaning carried in the medium are the result of brilliant perception. Like Howells' style, Smith's is very pure. Clarity and simplicity are as much artistic creations as are the baroque, or the elevated, or the effect of intensity; but richness of meaning that is managed in simplicity is rarer in the history of styles.

Independently, at about the same time as Rourke's study, H. L. Mencken's research led him to conclude that a stylistic revolution had been achieved early in the nineteenth century. The creators of this new ease, fullness, and flexibility in the American language were, Mencken asserted, the "lowely" newspaper humorists. It may be, then, that although Seba Smith's name was almost forgotten, as Miss Rourke says, his style can be regarded as a dominant creative achievement in the development of a distinctive American literary language.

In 1937 Walter Blair's *Native American Humor (1800 - 1900)* traced "the mutations of nineteenth century humorous treatments of American characters." Including a long introductory essay, a selected bibliography, and a large anthology, this work of creative scholarship established the artistic validity and the canon of American humor for generations of scholars throughout the United States. Blair's emphasis is on the antecedents and continuity of Jack as a type figure. His anthology devotes over twenty-five pages to Smith's Downing letters.

Later, in *Horse Sense in American Humor* (1942), Blair devoted a carefully analytic chapter to Jack Downing in which he observed for the first time that Jack as a literary character was a full development, sometimes wise, sometimes foolish: "like most men, he was neither an angel nor a devil, but a mixture of both, quaint and human and lovable." Blair was also the first to indicate that the country dialect offered by Davis' J. Downing, Major, was less lifelike than Smith's and that Davis' character was not "as rich a mixture of simplicity and wisdom as Jack," because Davis' use of the figure was simply for political ends. Finally, Blair points out that the late Jack Downing letters are more clearly partisan and satiric than the first series. This brief essay in literary evaluation is the most balanced reading of Jack's character available.

Harold W. Thompson devotes two compact and perceptive pages to Seba Smith's work in the *Literary History of the United States* (1949). Although Smith's work is not so frequently reprinted in the 1950's and 1960's as that of such Southwestern humorists as A. B. Longstreet, Johnson J. Hooper, T. B. Thorpe, or George Washington Harris, it is included in some anthologies. Kenneth S. Lynn's *The Comic Tradition in America* (1958) includes three pages of scholarly introduction and three letters. Lynn, following Tandy, believes Davis is "gifted with a keener sense of humor than Smith"; but he says that his character lacks "the tangy Maine flavor of the original." Walter Blair, Theodore Hornberger, Randall Stewart, and James Miller's two-volume college anthology, *The Literature of the United States*, has, in its various editions, richly represented the American humorists; and this work includes an introduction to and selections from Seba Smith.

IV   *The Historical Perspective*

Modern historians, interested in the growth and power of national images, have found in Jack Downing a figure to study for the sources of energies in broad historical movements and in national yearnings. John William Ward's *Andrew Jackson: Symbol for an Age* (1955) is an elegant example of such creative investigation. While Ward follows Tandy in calling Jack an "unlettered philosopher," he sees this quality as a popular misconception reflecting "the American emphasis on the sagacity of the common man." Grasping Smith as "a conservative, clinging to the established order," Ward continues perceptively: "But his object in creating the homely character, Jack Downing, was not to serve his social bias. It was to exploit his interest in the speech patterns and mores of the down-easterners among whom he had grown up. When Smith hit upon the idea of making his folk-hero an imaginary associate of Andrew Jackson, his treatment of the President, although humorously satirical, was tempered with a certain warmth and kindness." With this insight into Smith's devotion to the mores of down-Easterners, Ward can show the source not only of the warmth in Smith's treatment of Jackson, but also of delight that partisans of Jackson might take in Jack.

Daniel Hoffman's *Form and Fable in American Fiction* (1965), a study of themes and structures through examination of their sources in folklore, popular culture, and mythology, suggests the seminal position of Seba Smith. Locating Jack Downing among the mythic heroes of American innocence, Hoffman presents Jack as a version of pastoral:

> With the Rural Village as the locus of a paradisal symbolism in folklore and popular culture, we may well expect to find secular analogues to the Fall. Seba Smith achieved a delicate balance in Jack Downing between innocence and knowledge; his Major—his whole village of Downingville—has a knowledge which does not cost them their Down East paradise because it is instinctual knowledge, not the hard, mean knowledge gained by experience. Their innate good natures and their birthright of Yankee wisdom make such characters as Major Downing inviolable against chicanery.

Again we have a reading which does not deal with Smith's immediately reductive intent nor with the deeper problem of the weakness and destructiveness Smith saw in rural innocence when it is encouraged to form public policy. However, to see the pastoral symbolism in the grand tradition is to see the profoundest source of attraction in the character of Jack Downing and thus to share Seba Smith's vision of the cloudy glory of the Jacksonian revolution.

Jack Downing entered the national galaxy of vernacular characters as an ignorant, vital, sympathetically created figure. Through Jack's speech patterns, through his mores, and through the use of traditional themes and forms from folk humor, Smith provides a perspective which simultaneously reveals its own limitations and comically exposes absurdities in the standard culture and its institutions. His wife Elizabeth's hesitant question, "but is he not honest?," indicates the root ambiguity about the common man who is created almost wholly by his folk culture. Adventurous, generous, self-assertive, eager to rise but comically incompetent, he still exists in literature and in life as the hopeful, likeable American who expects to achieve, without painful effort, a marvelous fate.

The character is created in a style which is an even greater artistic achievement. Using dialect with tact and finesse, Seba Smith shaped in written form an easy and natural American colloquial speech. In his usage, the style becomes capable of complex comic and ironic nuances of meaning. For the first time in American literature, the vernacular perspective presents significant human, social, and political problems and relationships. Seba Smith's achievement in enlarging the use of the vernacular style is different in degree, not in kind, from Mark Twain's contribution. In the final analysis, Smith's claim to a modest place in the national literature is assured by his creation of the character of Jack Downing, the rich flavor of his down East local color, his wit as a political satirist, and the subtle and original skill with which he exploited the esthetic possibilities of the American language.

Notes and References

Chapter One

1. MS. Autobiography entitled "Class of 1818," Bowdoin College Library.
2. Mary Alice Wyman, *Two American Pioneers: Seba Smith and Elizabeth Oakes Smith* (New York, 1927), p. 2.
3. MS. Autobiography, Bowdoin.
4. The Bowdoin MS. Autobiography does not name the benefactor, but in a nearly identical document in the New York Public Library collection, Smith identifies him as Benjamin Tappan Chase. In the University of Virginia archives are several affectionate letters to Smith from Chase.
5. Cecil B. Williams, *Henry Wadsworth Longfellow* (New York, 1964), p. 32.
6. Henry James, *Hawthorne* (New York, 1879). Reprinted in Edmund Wilson, ed., *The Shock of Recognition* (New York, 1955), I, 441.
7. *Ibid.*, 442.
8. MS. Autobiography, Bowdoin.
9. *General Catalogue of Bowdoin College and the Medical School of Maine; a Biographical Record of Alumni and Officers, 1794 - 1950.* 5th ed. (Brunswick, Maine, 1950), p. 50.
10. Louis Clinton Hatch, *The History of Bowdoin College* (Portland, Maine, 1927), pp. 304 - 9.
11. Williams, pp. 35 - 36.
12. MS. Autobiography, Bowdoin. The address, "On the Equality with Which Nature Has Distributed the Means of Happiness," and a college essay, May, 1818, called "Disquisition on the Comparative Merits of Homer and Milton," are preserved in the Bowdoin College Library.
13. MS. Autobiography, Bowdoin. Letters, Benjamin T. Chase to Smith (in Charleston), February 1, 1820; Chase (in Baltimore), to Smith, May 6, 1820, University of Virginia Library.
14. Wyman, p. 14. Miss Wyman gives Elizabeth's birthplace as Yarmouth, but Smith says Cumberland in the MS. Autobiographies.
15. Letter from Smith to Rufus W. Griswold, August 11, 1842, New York Public Library, Manuscripts Division.
16. Seba to Elizabeth, October 31, 1833, University of Virginia Library.
17. Charles O. Stickney, "The Howitts of America," *Boston Evening Transcript* (May 28, 1894).

18. Seba to Elizabeth, November 30, 1865, University of Virginia Library.
19. Bowdoin College Library.
20. In the MS. Autobiographies (Bowdoin College and New York Public Library), Smith recalled that the *Courier* had been started in "the winter of 1830," but the first issue is dated October 13, 1829. See Wyman, p. 29, and Daniel Royot, "Publications de Seba Smith dans la presse de Portland-Maine de 1813 à 1836," an unpublished checklist in the authors' possession.
21. Wyman, p. 29.

Chapter Two

1. Cameron C. Nickels, "Seba Smith Embattled," *Maine Historical Society Quarterly*, XIII (1973), 8 - 18.
2. Seba Smith, *My Thirty Years Out of the Senate* (New York, 1859), pp. 36, 57, 60.
3. *Ibid.*, p. 5.
4. Wyman, pp. 35 - 36. For the Yankee in fiction, see V. L. O. Chittick, *Thomas Chandler Haliburton* (New York, 1924), pp. 360 - 67.
5. Wyman, p. 207, and Daniel Hoffman, *Form and Fable in American Fiction*, Galaxy ed. (New York, 1965), pp. 44 ff.
6. Elizabeth Hardwick, "Seduction and Betrayal," *The New York Review of Books* (June 14, 1973), p. 7.
7. Henry Nash Smith, *Mark Twain: The Development of a Writer* (Cambridge, Mass., 1962), p. viii.
8. *The Life and Writings of Major Jack Downing*, 3rd ed. (Boston, 1834), pp. 86, 125. Page references included in the text are to this edition, which contains one letter and at least five illustrations not in the first edition. The text of the second edition seems to be a reprint of the first.
9. Seba to Elizabeth, November 1, 1833, University of Virginia Library.
10. Letter from Elizabeth to Seba, June 4, 1837, University of Virginia Library.
11. R. W. B. Lewis, *The American Adam* (Chicago, 1955), p. 1.
12. Leo Marx, *The Machine in the Garden* (New York, 1967), p. 129.
13. Antti Aarne and Stith Thompson, *Types of the Folktale*, 2nd rev. ed. (Helsinki, 1964), 1525 n. For Rourke's discussion, see her p. 29.
14. Matthew Hodgart, *Satire* (New York, 1969), p. 23.
15. Mikhail Bakhtin, *Rabelais and His World*, trans. Helene Iswolsky (Cambridge, Mass., 1968), pp. 5 - 8, 11.
16. Miguel de Unamano, *The Life of Don Quixote and Sancho*, in *Our Lord Don Quixote*, trans. Anthony Kerrigan (Princeton, 1967), p. 264.
17. Bakhtin, p. 6.
18. *Ibid.*, pp. 10 - 12, 21.

19.   Carl G. Jung, "On the Psychology of the Trickster Figure," in Paul Radin, *The Trickster: A Study in American Indian Mythology* (New York, 1969), p. 200.

20.   Letter from Elizabeth to Seba, November 11, 1833, University of Virginia Library.

21.   H. L. Mencken, *The American Language: An Inquiry Into the Development of English in the United States* (New York, 1936), pp. 365 - 66. In *The American Language: Supplement II* (Boston, 1948) Mencken lists and evaluates the major studies of New England dialect.

22.   Workers of the Federal Writers' Project of the Works Progress Administration for the State of Maine, *Maine: A Guide "Down East,"* American Guide Series (Boston, 1937), pp. 76 - 78. Cited hereafter as *Maine: A Guide.*

23.   Ralph Waldo Emerson, "Ezra Ripley, D. D.," *Complete Works of R. W. Emerson* (Boston, 1892), X, 365.

24.   H. L. Mencken, *The American Language: Supplement I* (Boston, 1945), pp. 123 - 29.

25.   Walter Blair, *Mark Twain & Huck Finn* (Berkeley, 1962), pp. 240 - 48; Hennig Cohen and William B. Dillingham, *Humor of the Old Southwest* (Boston, 1964), p. 121.

Chapter Three

1.   Edward Pessen, *Jacksonian America* (Homewood, Ill., 1969), pp. 213, 326.

2.   Enid Welsford, *The Fool: His Social and Literary History* (Garden City, N.Y., 1961), p. 202.

3.   As Edgar G. Mouton, Jr., Louisiana State Senator, puts it, "It is not unusual to find 'resolutions' being introduced toward the end of the session that may deal with peculiar and unusual events that have arisen during the session and dealing with them in a joking manner, which, after much discussion, will be withdrawn." Letter to the authors, August 4, 1969.

4.   Quoted from Pessen, pp. 336 - 37.

5.   See Arthur M. Schlesinger, Jr., *The Age of Jackson* (Boston, 1945), p. 54; and Pessen, pp. 309 - 10 for a sympathetic and a revisionist assessment of the Peggy Eaton affair.

Chapter Four

1.   Alexis de Tocqueville, *Democracy in America*, trans. Henry Reeve, ed. Phillips Bradley (New York, 1957), I, 299.

2.   See, for example, Pessen, p. 342.

3.   *Ibid.*, p. 175.

4.   William W. Freehling, *Prelude to Civil War* (New York, 1966), pp. xi, xii.

5.   Quoted from Freehling, p. 222.

6.   Freehling, pp. 222, 274 - 75, xii, 377.

7.   In addition to Freehling, p. 377, see Kenneth M. Stampp, *The Peculiar Institution* (New York, 1966).

8.   Glyndon G. Van Deusen, *The Jacksonian Era* (New York, 1959), p. 73.

9.   Jennette Tandy, *Crackerbox Philosophers in American Humor and Satire* (New York, 1964), p. 31. First ed. New York, 1925.

10. To this point see Joseph Campbell, *The Hero with a Thousand Faces* (New York, 1956), p. 15.

11. Marquis James, *The Life of Andrew Jackson* (Indianapolis and New York, 1938), p. 641.

12. Smith's restrained style and imagery contrast significantly with the packed, intense style of George Washington Harris, *Sut Lovingood* (New York, 1867).

13. John William Ward, *Andrew Jackson: Symbol for an Age* (New York, 1962), esp. Ch. VI.

14. *Ibid.*, p. 83.

15. Quoted from Ward, pp. 83 - 84.

16. Quoted from Ward, p. 86.

17. Josiah Quincy, *Figures of the Past*, quoted from Ward, p. 86.

18. Miguel de Unamuno, *The Life of Don Quixote and Sancho*, pp. 293 - 94.

19. Lilly & Wait to Seba Smith, 6 [?] January, 1834, University of Virginia Library.

20. Wyman, p. 70.

21. *Ibid.*, p. 73. For the Davis-Biddle relationship see James, *The Life of Andrew Jackson*, p. 658, and n. 39, pp. 877 - 78.

Chapter Five

1.   Lewis P. Simpson, *The Man of Letters in New England and the South* (Baton Rouge, 1973), p. 152.

2.   Letters, Lilly, Wait, Colman & Holden, Publishers; to Seba Smith; September 11, 1833 and September 18, 1833, University of Virginia Library.

3.   Richard M. Dorson, "Sam Patch, Jumping Hero," *New York Folklore Quarterly*, I (1945), 150.

4.   James Guimond, *The Art of William Carlos Williams* (Urbana, Ill., 1968), p. 171.

5.   See Stith Thompson, *Motif-Index of Folk-Literature*. Revised and enlarged ed., 6 vols. (Blomington, Ind., 1958), M 312.

6.   *Ibid.*, K 233.4. See also Richard M. Dorson, *Jonathan Draws the Long Bow* (Cambridge, Mass., 1946), p. 21.

7.   David Tatham, "A Note About David Claypoole Johnston," *The Courier* XXXIV (1970), 11.

8. Seba to Elizabeth, October 12, 1833, University of Virginia Library.
9. Seba to Elizabeth, October 20, 1833, University of Virginia Library.
10. Seba to Elizabeth, November 6, 1833, University of Virginia Library.
11. Elizabeth to Seba, November 11, 1833, University of Virginia Library.
12. William Murrell, *A History of American Graphic Humor* (New York, 1933), I, 124 - 27.
13. From Albert Mathews, "Uncle Sam," *Proceedings of the American Antiquarian Society*, XIX (1908), 45.
14. Murrell, I, 132.
15. Quoted from "Preface by the Publishers," in [Seba Smith], *May-Day in New-York* (New York, 1845), xxvi.
16. Wyman, pp. 47 - 51. See also Royot MS.
17. Wyman, p. 88.

Chapter Six

1. Crockett and exploiters of his name even capitalized on Jack's popularity by considering him as a real person and by representing Davy as dining, discussing politics, and carrying on a spirited correspondence with the Major in *An Account of Col. Crockett's Tour to The North and Down East* (Philadelphia, 1835), pp. 44 - 45, 52, 116, 217 - 29. See Chapter 8, note 2, below.
2. Wyman, p. 98, quoted from *Selections from the Autobiography of Elizabeth Oakes Smith* (Lewiston, Me., 1924), p. 73. The biographical materials in this section are based on Wyman, pp. 97 - 108, who relies heavily on Elizabeth's autobiography.
3. Pessen, p. 32.
4. James Grossman, *James Fenimore Cooper* (Stanford, Cal., 1967), p. 121.
5. Bakhtin, pp. 282 - 83.
6. George E. Woodberry, *America in Literature* (New York, 1903), p. 63.
7. Wyman, pp. 115, 121 - 22. Poe's review is in the December, 1845, *Godey's Lady's Book*. In his collected works, the "Minor Contemporaries" series includes essays on both Seba and Elizabeth.
8. Wyman, pp. 109 - 14.
9. Ralph Thompson, *American Literary Annuals & Gift Books, 1825 - 1865* (New York, 1936), p. 4.
10. *Ibid.*, p. 9.
11. *Ibid.*, pp. 148, 35, 115, 161, 120, 139, 117.
12. Wyman, pp. 127 - 28.
13. Frank Luther Mott, *A History of American Magazines*, Vol I: 1741 - 1850 (Cambridge, Mass., 1939), Vol. II: 1850 - 1865 (Cambridge, Mass., 1938).

14. Wyman, p. 147. Mott calls Elizabeth one of the "leading magazinists of the times," I, 743.

15. Wyman, p. 132. Quoted from R. H. Stoddard, *Recollections* (New York, 1903), pp. 35 - 36.

16. Wyman, pp. 139 - 41.

17. Mott, II, 185.

18. Wyman, p. 141.

19. Mott, II, 448 - 50.

Chapter Seven

1. By use of the unusual form "Sir John," the surname Smith is avoided in the poem, perhaps one more evidence of Seba's uneasiness about the name's lack of distinction. See above, Chapter 6, Section II.

2. Elizabeth Nitchie, "The Longer Narrative Poems of America: 1775 - 1875," *Sewanee Review*, XXVI (July, 1918), 295. Cited Wyman, p. 154.

3. Robert E. Spiller et al., eds., *Literary History of the United States* (New York, 1949), II, 646 - 47.

4. Albert Keiser, *The Indian in American Literature* (New York, 1933), pp. 8 - 9 and *passim*.

5. Wyman, pp. 151 - 55.

6. *Ibid.*, p. 153.

7. Charles Haywood, *A Bibliography of North American Folklore and Folksong*, 2nd rev. ed. (New York, 1961), II, 763.

8. *Ibid.*, II, 776.

9. A college essay by Smith, "Disquisition on the Comparative Merits of Homer and Milton" (Bowdoin College Library), indicates that he had studied the great epics with some care.

10. Poe's review of *Powhatan* appeared in *Graham's Magazine* (July, 1841) and is reprinted as "Seba Smith" in the "Minor Contemporaries" series in the collected works.

11. Wyman, p. 152.

12. Quotation from *Southern Literary Messenger*, VII (April, 1841), 344. Second review was in VII (July-August, 1841), 588 - 89.

13. Unidentified clipping, New York Public Library.

14. *New Yorker*, April 24, 1841, p. 88.

15. Rufus W. Griswold, *Prose Writers of America*, 4th ed. (Philadelphia, 1851), p. 34.

16. Henry R. Schoolcraft, *History, Condition, and Prospects of the American Indians* (Rochester, N.Y., 1851). See also letter from Mary Schoolcraft to Elizabeth, July 26, 1858, University of Virginia Library.

17. Wyman, p. 12.

18. MS. draft of a "Prefatory Note" to his collected poems, University of Virginia Library.

19. See above Chapter 3, Section II and Chapter 5, Section II.
20. A file of Smith's MS. poems and clippings in the New York Public Library has "Die sterbende Mutter in Schneesturm." An undated clipping in the University of Virginia collection, "Stories of Famous Poems, 52," gives the history of the poem. The same collection includes clippings of Smith's poems from *Town's Second Reader* and the *National Fifth Reader*.
21. Anon., "Notices of New Works," *Southern Literary Messenger*, VII (March, 1841), 247 - 48. It was sometimes called "Three Little Graves."
22. Smith's MS. draft of the poem, with a note about where he read the account, is in the University of Virginia Library.
23. See Harold W. Thompson, *Body, Boots and Britches: Folktales, Ballads, and Speech from Country New York* (New York, 1939), pp. 374 - 77. Alan Lomax, *The Folk Songs of North America* (Garden City, N.Y., 1960), pp. 80 - 81, 94 - 95, lists the major folklore collections that include the ballad. Phillips Barry, "Fair Charlotte," *Bulletin of the Folk-Song Society of the Northeast*, No. 8 (1934), 17 - 19. Charles O'Brien Kennedy, ed., *American Ballads* (Greenwich, Conn., 1952), pp. ii - iii, 128 - 30.
24. *Maine: A Guide*, p. 77.
25. Lomax, p. 80.
26. Leslie Fiedler, *Love and Death in the American Novel*, rev. ed. (New York, 1966), p. 267.
27. *Ibid.*, p. 268.
28. MS. Introduction, in the University of Virginia Library.
29. MS. Autobiography, Bowdoin College Library.
30. Letter from Smith to N. Cleveland, February 6, 1854, Bowdoin College Library.
31. The New York Public Library has MSS. of Smith's presentation letters, the correspondence with Auguste Comte, and part of the lecture on geometry.
32. Letter from Smith to John A. Parker, July 28, 1851, University of Virginia Library.
33. Letter from Smith to the President or Senior Professor at Yale College, August 11, 1848, New York Public Library.
34. Professor David Eugene Smith, quoted in Wyman, p. 159.
35. Professor Blumberg, Head, Department of Mathematics at the University of Southwestern Louisiana, holds the Ph. D. in mathematics from the University of Wisconsin (1970). He generously undertook this evaluation at the request of the authors.

Chapter Eight

1. Marquis James, p. 658.
2. [David Crockett], *An Account of Col. Crockett's Tour to The North and Down East* (Philadelphia, 1835), p. 47. Attributed to Crockett, the volume is an anonymously edited collection of newspaper clippings. See *A*

Narrative of the Life of David Crockett of Tennessee, ed. James A. Shackford and Stanley J. Folmsbee (Knoxville, 1973), pp. v, ix - xx.
   3.   *An Account of Col. Crockett's Tour to The North and Down East*, pp. 48 - 49.
   4.   Henry David Thoreau, *Walden*, Chapter 1: "Economy."
   5.   The quotation and the term *flitting day* are from Robert Chambers, *Book of Days* (Philadelphia, [1914]), I, 679. See also "Candlemas," *Encyclopedia of Religion and Ethics*, III, 189 - 93.
   6.   Chambers, I, 570 - 79.

Chapter Nine

   1.   Letter from Smith to N. Cleveland, February 6, 1854, Bowdoin College Library. In an 1858 letter in the same collection, Smith spells the name "Cleaveland."
   2.   This list is probably incomplete. Wyman omits the Cincinnati, 1857, edition. The publishers were Samson & Phillips in Boston, John E. Potter in Philadelphia, and J. C. Derby in Cincinnati. Page references are to the Philadelphia edition of 1854.
   3.   Wyman, p. 165.
   4.   Anon., "Editorial Notes," *Putnam's Monthly Magazine*, V (February, 1855), 218.
   5.   Anon., "Literary Notices," *Harper's New Monthly Magazine*, X (January, 1855), 283.
   6.   MS. Autobiography, Bowdoin College Library.
   7.   "Gleanings from Early New England History," *Southern Literary Messenger*, VI (January, 1840), 46 - 49.
   8.   "The General Court and Jane Andrews' Firkin of Butter," *Graham's Magazine*, October, 1847. Summarized in Wyman, pp. 114 - 15.
   9.   In *The Colloquial Style in America* (New York, 1966), 55 - 56, Richard Bridgman remarks that the *Boston Post* noted a similar contrast in a case involving attorney Rufus Choate, a florid speaker. It published the court proceedings in two columns entitled "Poetry by Mr. Choate" and "Prose by the Witness."
   10.   Richard M. Dorson, *Jonathan Draws the Long Bow* (Cambridge, Mass., 1946), p. 99.
   11.   *Ibid.*, p. 100.
   12.   Benjamin A. Botkin, ed., *A Treasury of New England Folklore* (New York, 1947), pp. 168 - 69, 717, 721 - 22.
   13.   Dorson, *Jonathan Draws the Long Bow*, pp. 99 - 100. For the history and significance of the *Spirit of the Times*, see Norris W. Yates, *William T. Porter and the SPIRIT OF THE TIMES: A Study of the Big Bear School of Humor* (Baton Rouge, 1957).
   14.   Mott, *A History of American Magazines*, I, 626. Wyman, p. 110, attributes the put-down to Poe.

15. "Editorial Notes," *Putnams*, V (February, 1855), 218 - 19.

16. Wyman, p. 113n.

17. Dorson, *Jonathan Draws the Long Bow*, p. 256.

18. Botkin, pp. 147 - 48.

19. Aarne and Thompson, *Types of the Folktale*, type 1525J.

20. Thompson, *Motif-Index of Folk-Literature*, motif E235.

21. Wyman, pp. 97 - 98.

22. Quoted in Ward, p. 37.

23. Wyman, p. 101.

24. Lester V. Berrey and Melvin van den Bark, *American Thesaurus of Slang* (New York, 1952).

25. For examples see Dorson, *Jonathan Draws the Long Bow*, p. 95; and Botkin, p. 180.

26. For the publication of this fine story, see Milton Rickels, *Thomas Bangs Thorpe: Humorist of the Old Southwest* (Baton Rouge, 1962), pp. 95ff. For later critical interpretations see Richard Slotkin, *Regeneration Through Violence* (Middletown, Conn., 1973), pp. 479 - 84; and J. A. Leo Lemay, "The Text, Tradition, and Themes of 'The Big Bear of Arkansas,' " *American Literature*, XLVII (November, 1975), 321 - 42.

27. T. B. Thorpe, *The Hive of the "Bee Hunter"* (New York, 1854), p. 74.

28. "Uncle Pete and the Bear," *Southern Literary Messenger*, V (June, 1839), 430 - 32. Smith's name does not appear; he is identified as "the author of the original 'Jack Downing' Letters."

29. *Maine: A Guide*, pp. 415, 78.

30. "Getting Over the Difficulty," *The Rover*, I (1843), 361 - 63.

31. Winston Weathers, "The Rhetoric of the Series," *Contemporary Essays on Style*, ed. Glen A. Love and Michael Payne (Glenview, Ill., 1969), pp. 23 - 26.

32. Botkin, p. 730.

33. *Ibid.*, p. 643.

34. William Wells Newell, *Games and Songs of American Children* (1883; rpt. New York, 1963), pp. 5 - 6 and games numbered 88, 97, 100, and 108.

35. Botkin, pp. 742 - 43.

36. *Ibid.*, p. 750.

37. Wyman, p. 113.

38. J. Frank Dobie, *Coronado's Children: Tales of Lost Mines and Buried Treasures of the Southwest* (New York, 1931), pp. x - xi.

39. *Maine: A Guide*, pp. 79, 212, 350.

40. Quoted in Botkin, pp. 732 - 33.

41. Quoted in Dorson, *Jonathan Draws the Long Bow*, p. 201.

42. Thompson, motifs B292.8, C401.3, D1314.2, D2135.3, D2141, F147.3, F564.1, G216, G303.3.3.1.1, G303.16.14.4, K218.2, N553.5, N555.1, N571.

43.   Botkin, p. 606: devil in form of big black dog; pp. 536, 543: use of mineral rod to find treasure. Dorson, pp. 54 - 56: devil associated with treasure; pp. 48 - 49: devil's nearness signified by terrific storm; pp. 201, 215: cites expression "money diggers"; p. 224: use of witch hazel crotch to find treasure and moves it if you speak. Whittier (Norman, Okla., 1969), pp. 66 - 67: bargaining with Old Nick for a treasure; pp. 52 - 53: Satan in the form of a huge black dog.

44.   Wyman, p. 163.

45.   Killis Campbell, "Miscellaneous Notes on Poe," *Modern Language Notes,* XXVIII (1913), 65.

46.   George C. Groce and David H. Wallace, *The New-York Historical Society's Dictionary of Artists in America* (New Haven, Conn., 1957), p. 479.

47.   Harriet Beecher Stowe, *Oldtown Folks* (1869) and *Oldtown Fireside Stories* (1872); Sarah Orne Jewett, *Deephaven* (1877) and *The Country of the Pointed Firs* (1896); Mary Wilkins Freeman, *A New England Nun and Other Stories* (1891).

Chapter Ten

1.   Gales and Seaton to Seba Smith, April 25, 1847, University of Virginia Library.

2.   Frank Luther Mott, *American Journalism* (New York, 1950), p. 176.

3.   Russel B. Nye, *This Almost Chosen People,* (East Lansing, Mich., 1966), pp. 264, 195 - 96.

4.   Bridgman, pp. 28 - 32, analyzes effects achieved by lists. His work illustrates stunningly the influence of the vernacular on American prose style and provides a model for what might be achieved by close attention to Smith's style. For a literary antecedent of the comically expanding series, see Polonius' list of play types, *Hamlet,* Act II, Scene ii.

5.   Randall Stewart, *Nathaniel Hawthorne* (New Haven, Conn., 1948), pp. 127 - 34.

6.   See Richard Hofstadter, *The American Political Tradition* (New York, 1948) for background. For a modern conservative's philosophic analysis of the common man, see José Ortega y Gasset, *The Revolt of the Masses* (New York, 1957), esp. Chs. 1, 6, and 7.

7.   Ortega y Gasset, p. 60.

8.   Wyman, p. 149.

9.   *Eastern Argus,* December 17, 1866. Clipping in the New York Public Library.

10.   Letter from Elizabeth to Mr. Hart, May 18, 1868, Pennsylvania Historical Society.

11.   Quoted in Charles O. Stickney, "The Howitts of America," *Boston Evening Transcript,* May 28, 1894. Clipping in the University of Virginia Library.

Chapter Eleven

1.   Addressee unnamed, August 6, 1852, Bowdoin College Library.
2.   Seba Smith to N. Cleveland, February 6, 1854, Bowdoin College Library.
3.   Wyman, pp. 233 - 36.
4.   See note 2 above.
5.   Wyman, p. 236.
6.   *Ibid.*, pp. 68 - 69, 233 - 37.
7.   *Ibid.*, p. 83.
8.   For a sympathetic treatment, see William Wolf, "Arkansan on Stage," *Arkansas Democrat Magazine* (May 8, 1966), pp. 2 - 3.
9.   Clippings, University of Virginia Library.
10.   Stephen Hess and Milton Kaplan, *The Ungentlemanly Art: A History of American Political Cartoons* (New York, 1968), pp. 38, 39, 66, 177.
11.   Quoted from Van Wyck Brooks, *The World of Washington Irving* (New York, 1944), p. 33n.
12.   For a fuller survey of Smith's English reception, see Clarence Gohdes, *American Literature in Nineteenth Century England* (Carbondale, Ill., 1944), pp. 71 - 81 and elsewhere.
13.   James C. Austin, *Artemus Ward*, (New York, 1964), p. 82.
14.   Walter Blair, *Mark Twain & Huck Finn* (Berkeley, 1962), p. 244. *Mark Twain's Notebooks & Journals*, ed. Frederick Anderson, Lin Salamo, and Bernard L. Stein (Berkeley, 1975), II (1877 - 1883), 363.
15.   Tandy, p. 32.
16.   Rourke, *American Humor*, pp. 31, 29.
17.   In Constance Rourke, *The Roots of American Culture* (New York, 1942), pp. 247 - 48.
18.   *Ibid.*, pp. 247 - 48.

Selected Bibliography

PRIMARY SOURCES

The following titles are selected, corrected, and rearranged from Mary Alice Wyman's bibliography in *Two American Pioneers*, which may be consulted for a full but not complete listing of Seba Smith's books and his magazine contributions. M. Daniel Royot's typescript list, "Publications de Seba Smith dans la presse de Portland-Maine de 1813 à 1836," is deposited in photocopy in the Bowdoin College Library.

1. Manuscripts

Important deposits of letters and manuscripts include the Elizabeth Oakes Smith Collection, University of Virginia Library; Papers of Seba Smith, the New York Public Library; the Bowdoin College Library holdings; and others.

2. Books

The Life and Writings of Major Jack Downing, of Downingville, Away Down East in the State of Maine. Written by Himself. Boston: Lilly, Wait, Colman, & Holden, 1833. The second edition, 1834, seems a reprint of the first. The third edition, 1834, adds a letter dated December 28, 1833, and six illustrations. It seems Smith's final form for the book.

John Smith's Letters with "Picters" to Match. New York: Samuel Colman, 1839.

Powhatan; A Metrical Romance, In Seven Cantos. By Seba Smith. New-York: Harper & Brothers, 1841.

May-Day in New-York: or House-Hunting and Moving; Illustrated and Explained in Letters to Aunt Keziah. By Major Jack Downing. New-York: Burgess, Stringer and Company, 1845. Same volume entitled *Jack Downing's Letters by Major Jack Downing* published in Philadelphia, 1845.

Dewdrops of the Nineteenth Century Gathered and Preserved in Their Brightness and Purity. By Seba Smith. New York: J. K. Wellman, 1846. For numerous reissues see Ralph Thompson, *American Literary Annuals & Gift Books 1825 - 1865* (New York, 1936), p. 117.

New Elements of Geometry. By Seba Smith. New York: George P. Putnam, 1850. London: Richard Bentley, 1850.

'Way Down East; or, Portraitures of Yankee Life. By Seba Smith. The Original Major Jack Downing. New York: Derby and Jackson, 1854. Boston: Samson and Phillips, 1854. Philadelphia: John E. Potter,

1854. Cincinnati: J. C. Derby, 1854. Later editions, various cities, 1855, 1859, 1860, 1876, and 1884.
My Thirty Years Out of the Senate. By Major Jack Downing. Illustrated with Sixty-Four Original and Characteristic Engravings on Wood. New York: Oaksmith & Company, 1859.

SECONDARY SOURCES

1. Biography
WYMAN, MARY ALICE. *Two American Pioneers: Seba Smith and Elizabeth Oakes Smith.* New York: Columbia University Press, 1927. Not analytical but factual and carefully researched. The only full study of the two writers.
NICKELS, CAMERON C. "Seba Smith Embattled," *Maine Historical Society Quarterly,* XIII (Summer, 1973), 7 - 27. Full scholarly treatment of two significant personal episodes in Smith's early journalistic career.

2. General Criticism
BIER, JESSE. *The Rise and Fall of American Humor.* New York: Holt, Rinehart and Winston, 1968. Showing only a casual, general reading of Seba Smith, this work observes, "Downing is confusedly both the comic fool and sage observer."
BLAIR, WALTER. *Horse Sense in American Humor.* Chicago: University of Chicago Press, 1942. Traces the tradition of homely wisdom in American literature. Has an excellent interpretive chapter about Jack Downing.
————. *Native American Humor.* San Francisco: Chandler Publishing Co., 1960. Originally appearing in 1937, this work includes a general discussion of Seba Smith, selections from the Downing letters, and an indispensable bibliography.
DORSON, RICHARD M. "The Identification of Folklore in American Literature," *Journal of American Folklore,* LXX (1957), 1 - 8. Reprinted in Dorson's *American Folklore and the Historian.* Chicago: University of Chicago Press, 1971. Places Smith among those American writers who are not folk artists but whose literary work is "striated with oral folk humor."
————. *Jonathan Draws The Long Bow.* Cambridge, Mass.: Harvard University Press, 1946. Authoritative collection of New England folktales; contains two items by Seba Smith.
EBY, CECIL D. "Yankee Humor" in Louis D. Rubin, Jr., ed. *The Comic Imagination in American Literature.* New Brunswick, N.J.: Rutgers University Press, 1973. Good, brief presentation of Jack Downing's political functions.
HOFFMAN, DANIEL *Form and Fable in American Fiction.* Galaxy ed., New York: Oxford University Press, 1965. Has numerous references to Jack Downing, who is located among American mythic heroes of innocence in a national version of pastoral.

MENCKEN, HENRY L. *The American Language. Supplement I.* New York: Alfred A. Knopf, 1945. Maintains that the "lowly" newspaper humorists "forced the seasoning of American writing . . . with the vernacular." Smith's pioneering achievement is briefly assessed.

MILLER, ALAN R. "America's First Political Satirist: Seba Smith of Maine." *Journalism Quarterly*, XLVII (Autumn, 1970), 488 - 92. Argues Smith was the first political satirist in United States journalism; characterizes his tone as gentle and subtle.

ROURKE, CONSTANCE. *American Humor: A Study of the National Character.* New York: Harcourt, Brace and Co., 1931. Sees Jack as a large national type, carefully characterized, evoking complex responses. Brilliant study of uses of humor.

_____. *The Roots of American Culture and Other Essays.* New York: Harcourt, Brace and Co., 1942. A posthumous volume, edited, with a preface by Van Wyck Brooks. Contains the most perceptive evaluation written on the qualities and the significance of Smith's prose style.

SMITH, HENRY LADD. "The Two Major Downings: Rivalry in Political Satire," *Journalism Quarterly*, XLI (Winter, 1964), 74 - 78, 127. Contrasts Smith's low-keyed, subtle, restrained humor with Davis' broader, coarser, and more biting lampoons.

TANDY, JENNETTE. *Crackerbox Philosophers in American Humor and Satire.* New York: Columbia University Press, 1925. Study of the "unlettered philosopher" in American humorous literature. Contains an uneven but valuable analysis of Smith and his best-known imitator, C. A. Davis.

THOMPSON, HAROLD W. "American Humor," in R. E. Spiller and others, *Literary History of the United States.* New York: The Macmillan Co., 1949. Excellent but brief analysis of Seba Smith's work, including his ballads.

_____. *Body, Boots & Britches.* Philadelphia: J. B. Lippincott, 1939. Valuable discussion of how "Fair Charlotte" passed into the folk tradition.

THORP, WILLARD. *American Humorists.* University of Minnesota Pamphlets on American Writers. Minneapolis: University of Minnesota Press, 1964. In three compact paragraphs assesses Smith's achievement in creating Jack Downing and places him in the humorous tradition.

WARD, JOHN WILLIAM. *Andrew Jackson: Symbol for an Age.* New York: Oxford University Press, 1955. Illuminating study from the historical perspective of a national heroic symbol, the volume contains a full, careful analysis of Smith's treatment of Andrew Jackson's receiving an honorary Harvard degree.

Workers of the Federal Writers' Project of the Works Progress Administration for the State of Maine. *Maine: A Guide "Down East."* American Guide Series. Boston: Houghton Mifflin Co., 1937. Although Smith is undervalued, the writers place him in his local context in this richly informative book.

YATES, NORRIS W. *William T. Porter and the Spirit of the Times.* Baton Rouge: Louisiana State University Press, 1957. Study of one of the nineteenth century's best humorous journals and of its influential editor; has several references to Seba Smith in the context of the *Spirit's* traditions.

Index

(Works by Smith are listed under his name)